# The Blackfeet

Indians of North America

Heritage Edition

Indians
of North
America

Heritage Edition

Indians
of North
America

# The Blackfeet

Theresa Jensen Lacey

Foreword by
Ada E. Deer
University of Wisconsin-Madison

CHELSEA HOUSE
PUBLISHERS
A Haights Cross Communications ◢ Company ®

Philadelphia

COVER: Backrest, Provincial Museum of Alberta, Canada.

**CHELSEA HOUSE PUBLISHERS**

VP, NEW PRODUCT DEVELOPMENT   Sally Cheney
DIRECTOR OF PRODUCTION   Kim Shinners
CREATIVE MANAGER   Takeshi Takahashi
MANUFACTURING MANAGER   Diann Grasse

**Staff for THE BLACKFEET**

EXECUTIVE EDITOR   Lee Marcott
EDITOR   Christian Green
PRODUCTION EDITOR   Bonnie Cohen
PHOTO EDITOR   Sarah Bloom
SERIES AND COVER DESIGNER   Keith Trego
LAYOUT   EJB Publishing Services

Original edition first published in 1995.

A Haights Cross Communications ✦ Company ®

www.chelseahouse.com

First Printing

9  8  7  6  5  4  3  2  1

Library of Congress Cataloging-in-Publication Data

Lacey, Theresa Jensen.
  The Blackfeet / Theresa Jensen Lacey.
    p. cm. — (Indians of North America)
  Includes bibliographical references and index.
  ISBN 0-7910-8596-1 (hard cover)
  1. Siksika Indians—Juvenile literature. 2. Kainah Indians—Juvenile literature. 3.
Piegan Indians—Juvenile literature. I. Title. II. Indians of North America
(Chelsea House Publishers)
  E99.S54L33 2005
  978.004'97352—dc22
                                    2005006513

# Contents

# Foreword

Ada E. Deer

American Indians are an integral part of our nation's life and history. Yet most Americans think of their Indian neighbors as stereotypes; they are woefully uninformed about them as fellow humans. They know little about the history, culture, and contributions of Native people. In this new millennium, it is essential for every American to know, understand, and share in our common heritage. The Cherokee teacher, the Mohawk steelworker, and the Ojibwe writer all express their tribal heritage while living in mainstream America.

The revised INDIANS OF NORTH AMERICA series, which focuses on some of the continent's larger tribes, provides the reader with an accurate perspective that will better equip him/her to live and work in today's world. Each tribe has a unique history and culture, and knowledge of individual tribes is essential to understanding the Indian experience.

Prior to the arrival of Columbus in 1492, scholars estimate the Native population north of the Rio Grande ranged from seven to twenty-five million people who spoke more than three hundred different languages. It has been estimated that ninety percent of the Native population was wiped out by disease, war, relocation, and starvation. Today there are more than 567 tribes, which have a total population of more than two million. When Columbus arrived in the Bahamas, the Arawak Indians greeted him with gifts, friendship, and hospitality. He noted their ignorance of guns and swords and wrote they could easily be overtaken with fifty men and made to do whatever he wished. This unresolved clash in perspectives continues to this day.

A holistic view recognizing the connections of all people, the land, and animals pervades the life and thinking of Native people. These core values—respect for each other and all living things; honoring the elders; caring, sharing, and living in balance with nature; and using not abusing the land and its resources—have sustained Native people for thousands of years.

American Indians are recognized in the U.S. Constitution. They are the only group in this country who has a distinctive *political* relationship with the federal government. This relationship is based on the U.S. Constitution, treaties, court decisions, and attorney-general opinions. Through the treaty process, millions of acres of land were ceded *to* the U.S. government *by* the tribes. In return, the United States agreed to provide protection, health care, education, and other services. All 377 treaties were broken by the United States. Yet treaties are the supreme law of the land as stated in the U.S. Constitution and are still valid. Treaties made more than one hundred years ago uphold tribal rights to hunt, fish, and gather.

Since 1778, when the first treaty was signed with the Lenni-Lenape, tribal sovereignty has been recognized and a government-to-government relationship was established. This concept of tribal power and authority has continuously been misunderstood by the general public and undermined by the states. In a series of court decisions in the 1830s, Chief Justice John Marshall described tribes as "domestic dependent nations." This status is not easily understood by most people and is rejected by state governments who often ignore and/or challenge tribal sovereignty. Sadly, many individual Indians and tribal governments do not understand the powers and limitations of tribal sovereignty. An overarching fact is that Congress has plenary, or absolute, power over Indians and can exercise this sweeping power at any time. Thus, sovereignty is tenuous.

Since the July 8, 1970, message President Richard Nixon issued to Congress in which he emphasized "self-determination without termination," tribes have re-emerged and have utilized the opportunities presented by the passage of major legislation such as the American Indian Tribal College Act (1971), Indian Education Act (1972), Indian Education and Self-Determination Act (1975), American Indian Health Care Improvement Act (1976), Indian Child Welfare Act (1978), American Indian Religious Freedom Act (1978), Indian Gaming Regulatory Act (1988), and Native American Graves Preservation and Repatriation Act (1990). Each of these laws has enabled tribes to exercise many facets of their sovereignty and consequently has resulted in many clashes and controversies with the states and the general public. However, tribes now have more access to and can afford attorneys to protect their rights and assets.

Under provisions of these laws, many Indian tribes reclaimed power over their children's education with the establishment of tribal schools and thirty-one tribal colleges. Many Indian children have been rescued from the foster-care system. More tribal people are freely practicing their traditional religions. Tribes with gaming revenue have raised their standard of living with improved housing, schools, health clinics, and other benefits. Ancestors' bones have been reclaimed and properly buried. All of these laws affect and involve the federal, state, and local governments as well as individual citizens.

Tribes are no longer people of the past. They are major players in today's economic and political arenas; contributing millions of dollars to the states under the gaming compacts and supporting political candidates. Each of the tribes in INDIANS OF NORTH AMERICA demonstrates remarkable endurance, strength, and adaptability. They are buying land, teaching their language and culture, and creating and expanding their economic base, while developing their people and making decisions for future generations. Tribes will continue to exist, survive, and thrive.

Ada E. Deer
University of Wisconsin–Madison
June 2004

# 1

# The Coming To Be of the Blackfeet

There are a number of creation myths told by Blackfeet elders, and here are two. This first one is more popular with contemporary Blackfeet, and is based on a version told by the respected elder Chewing Blackbones, who related this story to author Ella E. Clark:

Old Man came from the south. He made mountains, prairies, forests, birds and animals especially suited to live in their environment. After he finished creating everything, he rested, and where he rested, hills formed which you can see to this day. Old Man covered the plains with grass for the animals, and made other plants to grow such as carrots, turnips and sarvisberries. Then Old Man made the first people—a woman and child—out of clay. When they came to life, he told them his name was *Napi*, meaning Old Man. Napi showed the woman and child how to find and make food from all the living things, the plants and animals. He showed them how to make

1

A Blackfeet man watches the sun set. The sun plays a large part in Blackfeet lore and one of their creation stories purports that the sun was responsible for the creation of the earth, the moon, the Big Dipper, the weather, and night and day. The story also has many similarities to the Genesis account, which appears in Christian and Jewish scriptures.

bows and arrows to hunt the animals, and how to make fire to cook their flesh.

As Old Man continued his travels north, he made more people, so they would be spread out. He also made a special gift for his people: the buffalo, which would give the people every-thing they would need for food, clothing, and shelter. Before he left the people, Old Man told them he would always care for them and would come back for them.

The second story, from elder Percy Bullchild, goes something like this: Once, a long time ago, the only living thing was *Creator Sun*, who has been here since time began and will never die. Creator Sun became quite lonely and decided to use his substantial powers to make companions. He spat upon some space dust and made a ball of mud, which became the earth. From some of the earth's dust, Creator Sun made a snake, which multiplied itself until there were so many snakes that Creator Sun decided to make the Earth boil and to make lava flow in order to kill the snakes. Only one snake, a female about to bear young, survived.

After this experiment, Creator Sun longed for a mate and decided to create the Moon. Their union was a fruitful one, and the Moon gave birth to seven sons. Creator Sun and his family were happy until one of the sons of the surviving snake, called Snakeman, changed his form into that of a man and became the Moon's secret love. When Creator Sun discovered the affair he flew into a rage, and he and his seven sons killed Snakeman and the Moon and burned their bodies until all that was left were some ashes.

Despite the Moon's death, Creator Sun realized that she would return somehow to avenge her lover's death, so he prepared his sons for trouble. He gave each of them a tool that they could use to defend themselves against the Moon when she returned. To the youngest son, called Rawman because he was so pink when he was born, Creator Sun gave a bladder of water. The second youngest son was given a bird; the next son, a bladder of air. To the fourth youngest son, the father gave a stick. The fifth was given a small rock; the sixth, some magic powers in his fingers. The eldest son, like Rawman, also received a bladder of water.

From the ashes of the fire used to burn the Moon's and Snakeman's bodies, a spark of what was left of the Moon flew out into the sky, and she lived once again in her old form. In a murderous rage, she immediately went to her sons' camp to kill her children. The sons ran from her, using the things their father had given them in order to try and slow her down. The eldest son threw his water bladder at her and caused rain to fall upon her. The sixth son drew a line in the dirt with his finger and created canyons and steep valleys. The son with the rock threw it and made high mountains. The fourth son, who had a stick, threw that down and caused dense forests to grow. The third son threw his bladder of air and made great winds blow all around the Moon. The son with the beautiful, multicolored bird threw it into the air; the bird became the first thunder and lightning. With his bladder of water, Rawman caused a great flood to form around his mother.

These obstacles slowed the Moon momentarily, but she continued her pursuit. Just as she reached Rawman, screaming death threats, Creator Sun threw his hatchet at her and cut off her leg. The sons escaped, and the Moon spent four days mending her leg, which was never quite the same again.

The sons and their father became airborne and flew up into the sky. The Moon followed, and they are all still in the sky today. The seven sons became the stars that make up the Big Dipper. They and their father, Creator Sun, are always just ahead of the Moon, and because the seven sons still throw things at the Moon to slow her down, weather of all types comes to the Earth from the sky.

In order to hide from the Moon, Creator Sun made day and night. The Moon is kept in the darkness so that she cannot see her sons very well. To punish all the snakes in the world for this trouble, Creator Sun made them to be despised by all others in creation. The Moon was also punished, being left completely bare, with an inhospitable climate and no life forms on her or in her. In addition, Creator Sun caused the Moon to be invisible for several days of the month.

After this disastrous experience with the Moon, Creator

Sun decided the Earth would make a better wife. Under the never-ending light of Creator Sun, Mother Earth produced all other life forms. But the snakes living on Mother Earth were still hostile to Creator Sun, and some of them changed into huge reptiles and dinosaurs, and disobeyed Creator Sun's laws. He destroyed the rebellious animals with a great flood, sparing only the smaller snakes; the remains of these gigantic creatures are excavated by *archaeologists* today.

Creator Sun then took some mud and made the first man, breathing life into him and calling him Mudman. After a while, Creator Sun noticed that Mudman was lonely. Finding Mudman asleep one day, Creator Sun made Mudman fall into an even deeper sleep, took his smallest rib, and made a woman, Ribwoman, to be his companion. Mudman and Ribwoman began to have children, and they eventually had so many that some of them had to leave and make camps of their own, so that there would be enough food for them all. The children traveled in the four cardinal directions of north, south, east, and west, and they further multiplied, populating the Earth. They spread out so far from one another that their one shared language began to change, becoming many languages. But no matter what language they speak, all humans today are related, being the descendants of Mudman and Ribwoman, and they are all nurtured by the light of Creator Sun, who is everywhere.

Unfortunately, the people were not always well. If they ate the wrong thing by accident, they would become ill, and sometimes, they were in pain. Creator Sun felt bad, seeing so many of his people, especially the children, getting sick and dying. He came to Earth, took Mudman with him into the forests and fields, and showed him the healing powers of certain herbs and barks. He also showed him what saps, berries, and roots he could use for medicine, for both outside and inside the body. Creator Sun taught Mudman how to take *sweat baths* to purify himself and how to paint his face and body to protect himself from harm.

Creator Sun also taught Mudman how to seek the spirits by going on a *vision quest* in order to gain power from the spirit world. These instructions were passed on from Mudman to the people, and those who practiced this wisdom became known as medicine men or *shamans*. Medicine men can never ask for pay in return for healing someone, because it was not Creator Sun's intention that this knowledge be hoarded.

## The Blackfeet:
### The Creation Myth and World Religions

You may notice some similarities between the "mainstream" Christian stories of how the earth was created, the waters formed, and living things animated, and the stories from the Blackfeet people. Their creation story also tells of a snake being the cause of so much trouble from the beginning, of a great flood, of the first man being created from the dust of the earth, and of woman being created from man's rib. The creation story also shares the similarity of the first woman's choice in causing all life-forms to eventually perish (similar to the story of Eve and the apple).

As similar as these stories are, there are differences between Native American religious cultures and those brought here from other continents. The most striking difference is that the First People do not distinguish between the supernatural and the natural; the material and spiritual worlds are part of a holistic realm. While most "mainstream" faiths perceive a kind of divide between heavenly and worldly beings, this gulf is not a part of the Blackfeet (and Native American in general) religious view.

In his book, *Man's Rise to Civilization as Shown by the Indians of North America from Primeval Times to the Coming of the Industrial State* (New York: Dutton, 1968), Peter Farb writes that the process of Christian "conversion" among Native Americans was not a giving in of one faith to relinquish the original one. Rather, he says that in a process termed *religious syncretism*, the First People often simply took what appealed to them from the "new" faith, whether it was Protestant or Catholicism (or, sometimes, both), and intermixed the elements of Christian faith with their own.

This is one variant of the Blackfeet creation myth. The creation myth was passed on through the telling of stories, and there are numerous modifications of this myth, which often changes from place to place or from generation to generation. Another version of the creation myth states that the first people created were a woman and a child, who were first made of mud and then given the power of speech. The woman immediately began to ask questions, asking the creator what form she and the child were before they were made to live, and then asking him if she and the child would ever stop living. The creator had not yet considered the latter question, so he picked up a buffalo chip (a dried piece of buffalo dung) and told the woman that he would throw it into a lake; if the chip floated, then the people would live forever. The woman was new to life and did not yet know what would and what would not float in water, so she stopped him, pointing out that the buffalo chip would dissolve in the water, and asked him to throw in a stone instead. The stone, of course, sank the instant it was thrown in, and the creator informed the woman that she had just made the decision for all life forms to eventually perish.

This is one of the myths of one of the most powerful Native American *tribes* still in existence today, the Blackfeet Nation. The Blackfeet Nation includes three divisions: the Siksikas (the Blackfeet proper); the Bloods, or Kainahs (Many Chiefs); and the Pikunis (The Poorly Dressed Ones), Piegans, or Peigans. The traditional territory of the Blackfeet spanned the U.S.–Canadian border, so with the establishment of separate *reservations* in Canada and the United States, the Piegans were further divided into the Canadian North Piegans and the American South Piegans. The name *blackfeet* came from the color of the soles of the moccasins worn by tribe members; these soles were darkened either with paint or from walking over burnt prairie grasses. The term was probably not used to indicate people outside the Siksika division before the arrival of the whites. Since the three divisions are culturally and linguistically identical and often fought together as allies, white observers used the name Blackfeet to designate people from all three divisions. Present-day Blackfeet reside in Siksika, Kainah, and Piegan reserves in Alberta, Canada, but the majority now live on the Blackfeet Reservation near Browning, Montana.

The history of the Blackfeet, like that of Native American peoples as a whole, was passed orally from one generation to the next. Because of this oral tradition, stories that are considered historical by contemporary society are blended with stories that are considered mythical. As a result, not much is known about the history of the Blackfeet before they came into contact with Europeans. There are, however, many theories and explanations as to how the Blackfeet and other Native Americans arrived on the continent of North America.

Most historians and scientists agree that the majority of Native Americans migrated from Asia. Long ago, a slender thread of land crossed the Bering Sea, which separates what is now known as Siberia and Alaska, bringing together the Asian and North American continents. On a great migration that was to last at least a thousand years, the prehistoric Native Americans traversed the land bridge across the Bering Strait and settled on this continent.

Further evidence in support of this theory was provided in 1991 by a study conducted by a biochemist named Douglas C. Wallace at Emory University in Atlanta, Georgia. Wallace took blood samples from ninety-nine different people from three geographically disparate groups of Indians: the Ticunas of South America, the Mayas of Central America, and the Pimas of North America. Wallace detected rare chemical sequences in the mitochondrial DNA of the samples and found that these sequences occurred only in the DNA of Asian populations. The obvious conclusion is that the Indians occupying the American continent originally came from Asia. Wallace did not find this chemical sequence in Eskimos, Navajos, Aleuts, and other tribes who, he theorized, arrived here at a later date. Wallace also claimed that he was able to trace the DNA lineages of these tribes to at least four women in an early migrating group, and similar studies published in more recent years confirmed Wallace's original findings.

On the basis of this shared mitochondrial DNA, Wallace theorized that the Bering Strait trek first occurred fifteen to thirty thousand years ago. There are conflicting hypotheses, however. Geneticist Svante Paabo of the University of California–Berkeley, recently argued against some of Wallace's findings. Paabo claimed that the tribes of the Pacific Northwest have thirty, rather than four, different mitochondrial DNA sequences in common, which would place the crossing of the Bering Strait at a much earlier date, forty to fifty thousand years ago. Whenever they arrived, the predecessors of present-day Native Americans began settling in and multiplying on the continent that is now North America.

From the Bering Strait, the ancestors of the Blackfeet most probably traveled south, then turned east and north. Researchers believe this to be true because the Blackfeet are part of the Algonquin group of tribes, which are linguistically related. These tribes inhabited an area ranging from Labrador in the North to the Carolinas in the South to the Great Plains in the West. In addition to being Algonquin, the Blackfeet are among the group of tribes known as the Plains Indians, which also includes the Sioux, Crow, Kiowa, Arikara, Pawnee, Nez Perce, Cheyenne, Cree, and Gros Ventre. Although they sometimes traded together, often warred against each other, and shared certain elements of their *cultures*, the Plains Indians are not a culturally homogenous group but are grouped together because they shared a particular geographic area, namely the Great Plains.

Before the advent of the horse, the Blackfeet probably lived on the plains in the northwestern area of what is now the province of Saskatchewan. They were probably hunter-gatherers; unlike some other Plains tribes, there is no indication that

The Blackfeet are believed to have originally inhabited the area north of the Great Lakes, but by the time Europeans arrived in the 1600s, the tribe began moving west, settling in the area of the northern Rocky Mountains, in what is now northwestern Montana and southern Alberta. Shown here is a small Blackfeet encampment at the foot of the Rockies.

the Blackfeet cultivated any crops (except perhaps tobacco) before they discovered horses. Once the horse increased their military capability, the Blackfeet displaced other tribes and settled in the fertile foothills of the Rocky Mountains, in the northwest corner of the Great Plains. The Rockies gave the Blackfeet a natural boundary to their territory and offered them a degree of protection from surprise attacks. The lush hillsides supported plants and trees of all types, such as cedars, spruces, hemlocks, pines, and Douglas firs. The valleys at the base of the mountains had an abundance of rich soil and clear, running streams.

But the area also had its natural hazards. The vast Sea of Grass (as the Blackfeet called the Great Plains) was ruled by quicksilver weather conditions ranging from violent prairie storms or bone-cracking cold winds to still, hot days that might only be relieved by pounding hailstorms and heart-stopping flash floods. Despite the harsh weather, the wealth and diversity of the land attracted many species of wildlife, many of which are now rare, endangered, or extinct. There were several hundred species of birds, including the red trumpeter swan. The mountains and waters teemed with beaver, mink, deer, and fox, while the plains were covered with enormous herds of buffalo.

Blackfeet territory also contained another form of wealth, one that existed beneath the earth. The Blackfeet did not mine or use metal before the coming of the Europeans and were unaware that their mountains were rich in gold, silver, copper, and coal. Unfortunately, this mineral wealth attracted white settlers and was the determining factor in the U.S. government's decision to restrict the Blackfeet to a reservation only a fraction of the size of the territory they ordinarily traversed in an endless search for plunder and buffalo.

# 2

# Shall Be Peeled and Elk Dog

O f all the animals that inhabited the fertile plains and foothills of Blackfeet territory, the one that was most important to the survival and lifestyle of the Blackfeet (and the Plains Indians as a whole) was the bison, or buffalo. Before its near extermination by white hunters, the buffalo population in North America numbered in the millions. The enormous beasts ranged from the Rocky Mountains to the eastern woodlands in herds so large that it would sometimes take hours for a herd to cross a stream. The Blackfeet called the buffalo *eye-i-in-nawhw*, which means "shall be peeled," a reference to the fact that the buffalo was "peeled" (skinned) before it was butchered and eaten.

The buffalo herds were not only a cornerstone of life for the Plains Indians; they symbolized their very existence and freedom and were viewed as a special gift from Creator Sun. According to one Blackfeet legend, Creator Sun, who always kept a watchful eye upon all he had created, saw that the people began to grow thin even though he had given them many different kinds of herbs and other vegetation to eat. He made a four-legged creature from the mud and blew life into the creature's nostrils. Then, as he did with Mudman, Creator Sun caused the animal to fall into a deep sleep. He removed the small rib from the animal and made a mate for it, thus creating the first male and female buffalo. The people began to fill out when they had this "flesh food," or meat, to eat. Creator Sun then made all the other animals: animals and birds to be eaten and animals and birds of prey. The former were to give the people food; the latter, to keep the former's population at a manageable level. Creator Sun also told the Blackfeet that if they would use all they could from each edible animal, and not ever waste, then they would never go hungry again.

For the Blackfeet and other Plains tribes, the buffalo was tangible proof that their creator provided and cared for them, because the buffalo supplied them with virtually everything they needed. The Blackfeet wasted no part of the buffalo, because it was a divine gift. To waste it would not only be foolish but would be a sign of ingratitude to their creator. Each part of the animal had a use, and often more than one. For example, the hide could be scraped clean and tanned with a mixture of buffalo brains, liver, and fat, and used to make robes, caps, leggings, shirts, coats, dresses, belts, moccasins, breechcloths, underwear (made from soft calfskin), and an envelope-like bag called a parfleche used to carry dried foodstuffs. Hides with the hair left on were useful in making winter clothing, and hides that were waterproofed by being smoked over a fire made durable tepees. Rawhide became tools such as pole hitches, horseshoes, blankets, and shields. Hair was used for stuffing pillows, padding saddles, and making ropes, headdresses, and ornaments. Horns made headdress ornaments, masks that protected horses in battle, powder flasks, spoons, cups, ladles, and ceremonial rattles,

Like all Plains Indians, the Blackfeet's way of life largely revolved around the buffalo, which provided clothing, shelter, and sustenance. The hides of these animals were tanned and made into robes, caps, leggings, shirts, coats, dresses, belts, and moccasins. The man in the center of this photo is wearing a rawhide coat made from a buffalo hide.

while bones were made into gaming dice, arrowheads, hide scrapers, knives, and sewing awls. Tendons made fine thread for sewing clothing and tepee covers and could be used to make strings for bows. The four-chambered stomach lining was cut up to make shoes or clothing or was kept whole and used as a cooking vessel or a water bag. Hooves were made into rattles and glue, and even buffalo chips were used to fuel fires and also served as an excellent mosquito repellent when crumbled and rubbed onto the skin.

Everything edible on the buffalo was consumed. The hump and tongue of the animal were considered delicacies, and the liver was often eaten immediately after making a kill. Tougher parts of the animal were cut in strips and dried to make jerky; this jerky could be ground with stones and mixed with berries and buffalo fat to make pemmican, a lightweight food that resisted spoilage and was used when traveling or when fresh meat was not available.

Since the buffalo was so essential to Blackfeet life, Blackfeet hunters carefully studied its life cycle. The Blackfeet called buffalo of different ages and sexes by different names; for example, a six-year-old, fully mature female buffalo was called "Big Female," while a six-year-old bull was called "Horns Not Cracked," because his horns were usually polished and smooth. The age of the buffalo determined its use, and sometimes whether it was to be killed at all. Older buffalo tended to have tough meat and rough, wrinkled, battered hides; consequently, they were usually left alone. In contrast, calves had distinctive yellow or reddish hair for several months after birth, so their hides were harvested to make children's robes. The best hides came from the four-year-old calves, which were hunted in January and February, when their hair was very silky and thick, like fine fur.

But the buffalo was not simply valued as a source of food and clothing. Children of promise were given names that related to the buffalo, and if a warrior or hunter had brought great honor to his people, his name would be changed to include the word for buffalo. Much of Blackfeet religion centered on the buffalo; medicine men prayed to the buffalo as the intermediary between themselves and the creator, and many items used in religious ceremonies, from masks and headdresses to ceremonial rattles, were made from buffalo parts. Buffalo skulls were used in almost all important religious ceremonies, and medicine bundles, used to cast spells or for personal protection, always included some part of the buffalo.

Blackfeet holy men had several rites for enticing buffalo to come near the hunting camps, because prior to the horse, buffalo herds had to be within walking distance of a camp in order to be hunted. In one holy rite, a holy man who owned a unique stone (called a buffalo stone because of its shape) would hold a ceremony in his tepee along with a number of hunters of renown and would call the buffalo using the magical stone. Buffalo hairballs found on the prairie were also used in ceremonies to attract the animals, as were special songs. Holy men would also have dreams or hold *esoteric* rituals that would tell them where the buffalo could be found. The Blackfeet also used a less spiritual method to attract buffalo: each spring they burned old, tough prairie grass to encourage the growth of tender, tasty, new grass.

Once a herd was discovered by scouts, a well-organized hunting party set out after them. Certain young hunters were given the special task (considered a great honor) of providing meat for someone who had no provider, such as a widowed woman and her children or elders who could not hunt for themselves. The hunting party was followed by the women and children, who carried the implements necessary to dress and transport the kill. Since at the slightest sign of danger a herd of buffalo will stampede, often not stopping until miles away, the Blackfeet had strict rules on how the hunt should proceed. Most important, no one was allowed to hunt alone, because although one or two hunters might bring down a couple of buffalo, in doing so they would frighten away the rest of the herd, and driving away game was considered criminal. Discipline during the hunt was so important that a small *band* of Blackfeet were deployed to keep the hunt in good order and observe the activities of the hunters. The hunters would stalk the buffalo, sneaking quietly up to a chosen beast and kill it with arrows. The hunters would decorate their arrowheads with an identifying design so that the women butchering the buffalo could accurately identify what kill belonged to whom.

Often hunters camouflaged themselves with wolf skins when stalking buffalo. Buffalo, being much larger than wolves, were not afraid of them, and the disguised hunters could creep

## The Buffalo:
### A Continuing Legacy on Hooves

The Blackfeet, like all Plains Indians, revered the buffalo (properly known as bison) as a symbol of freedom and a way of life. Although much has changed since the Blackfeet roamed freely on the Great Plains, the buffalo remain a source of interest to many people and continue to be revered by all Native Americans.

More than an estimated 60 million buffalo were slaughtered by white hunters—most between the 1830s and 1860s and largely due to the great demand for their hides—and for a time the species' very survival hung in a delicate balance. Although the buffalo are no longer endangered, they often roam outside of National Parks and onto ranches, where many farmers have slaughtered trespassing buffalo in an attempt to protect their own herds of cattle from diseases some buffalo carry, such as brucellosis and tuberculosis (but in spite of testing, no buffalo has ever tested positive for such diseases).

To establish healthy buffalo populations on tribal lands, thereby also establishing hope for the future of Native American people, the InterTribal Bison Cooperative (ITBC) was established in 1990. In a cooperative effort with the Native American Fish and Wildlife Society, the ITBC was formed to assist tribes with bison programs. As a result of this inter-tribal effort, in June 1991 Congress appropriated funds for tribal bison programs. Now the ITBC is a non-profit intertribal organization. There are forty-two tribes involved in ITBC and they have a collective herd of nearly ten thousand bison. The organization, headquartered in South Dakota, also actively works with the National Park Service and other U.S. government agencies, to help protect bison herds on those lands.

Prior to the twentieth century, the Blackfeet moved from camp to camp, depending on the season and availability of food. One of the most important means of transporting large amounts of goods was through the use of a travois (shown here). The travois was a simple contraption, which held household items, weapons, and food, and was made by joining two long poles with a type of netting in between.

up to a herd without causing a stampede. Hunters discarded their bows and arrows for another type of stalking where they would don buffalo skins, stand next to a cliff, and imitate a buffalo's call—usually that of a buffalo cow. The buffalo, which have very poor eyesight, would follow the call and could be easily lured over the cliff's edge. If there was a large herd of buffalo near a cliff, their tendency to stampede could be used against them. The entire tribe would gather quietly downwind from a herd. On a given signal, they would shout and wave cloths or flaming torches to alarm the herd and cause them to stampede over the edge to their deaths. If any buffalos survived the fall, they were dispatched by hunters with lances waiting below. When lakes would freeze in winter, the

Blackfeet would sometimes drive the buffalo onto the ice. Their weight would break the ice, and the hapless animals would founder in the cold water. Even if the buffalo did not break through the ice, they were not surefooted enough to remain standing for long. Either way, they were easy to finish off with lances, or later, guns.

Because of the migratory nature of the buffalo, travel was a central aspect of Blackfeet life. The Blackfeet never established permanent villages, using camps instead, and everything they made or owned could be quickly packed and easily carried. Their homes, tentlike structures called tepees, were lightweight and could be assembled, disassembled, and carried with relative ease. Tepees had frames made of long wooden poles and walls made of waterproof buffalo skins. When one was dismantled for travel, the tepee was lashed to a sledlike vehicle called a *travois*, which also carried the Blackfeet's possessions. Originally, these travois were pulled by dogs (which were considered more as work animals than pets), but since a dog could only carry about fifty pounds or pull about seventy-five pounds, people usually had to carry a part of the load themselves. In addition, young children had to be carried by an adult or had to walk, which slowed progress on the trail.

All this changed with the introduction of the horse to the Blackfeet. Indeed, the horse, called Big Dog or Elk Dog, had an impact on Blackfeet life that was almost as profound as that of the buffalo. Although most historians agree that the horse was introduced to North America by Spanish conquistadores, the Blackfeet have their own explanation. According to Blackfeet myth, the horse was brought to the Blackfeet by a brave named Long Arrow. Long Arrow was an orphan and was for a long time the scorn of his tribe. Finally, his chief, Good Running, took pity on him and adopted him. He matured into a handsome brave and became a fine hunter, but he always remained troubled by the fact that the tribe remembered him as an outcast. Long Arrow decided to do something of such importance that his people would forget the time when they scorned him and would remember only the great things he did.

When he discussed this decision with Good Running, the chief told him of a legendary spirit tribe who was said to live in the bottom of a lake far away and to keep strange animals who were larger than elk but who worked for people, like dogs. These animals were called *pono-kamita*, or Elk Dogs. Good Running told Long Arrow that many generations of young warriors had gone in search of these Elk Dogs, but none of them had ever come back. Long Arrow decided he would go and try to find them.

The people of the tribe prepared Long Arrow for his dangerous mission. First he was purified by a sweat bath (a religious ceremony wherein individuals congregated to pray and meditate in a heated lodge filled with steam), then he learned how to use a pipe and was taught useful prayers. A shaman gave him "medicine" (a sort of good luck charm) and a painted shield, which had designs on it to protect him. Good Running gave his son his own bow and one final sweat bath before Long Arrow left early one morning.

Long Arrow traveled south until he came to a pond. The spirit of the pond appeared in the shape of a man. He told Long Arrow that he might find the Elk Dogs if he would speak with the spirit's uncle, who lived in a large lake four times four days' journey away. (Four is a sacred number among many Plains tribes.) Long Arrow walked south for sixteen more days, through rough terrain and in bad weather, dry and cold. He finally came to a large lake and found himself facing a spirit-man twice the height of a normal man. The tall spirit menaced Long Arrow, but the young brave showed himself to be unafraid, and the tall spirit decided to help him, telling him to find the grandfather-spirit, who was yet another four times four days' worth of travel away.

At the end of this time, Long Arrow came to a lake of fantastic size, with snowcapped mountains ringing it. He knew that he must be in the right place and was so exhausted that he collapsed into a deep sleep. He awoke to find a small, beautifully dressed boy standing beside him. The boy told Long Arrow to get up and to follow him down to the bottom of the lake. Long Arrow did so, and found that not only could he breathe underwater, he did not even get wet.

Long Arrow followed the boy to the bottom of the lake, where he found a tepee. Inside the tepee, Long Arrow met the boy's grandfather, who was very powerful and magical. After eating with Long Arrow, sharing a pipe, and praying together, the old man had his grandson show Long Arrow the Elk Dogs. The boy taught Long Arrow how to ride an Elk Dog, and the young brave discovered the exhilaration of riding on the back of one of the beautiful, swift, sleek animals.

Before going back in the tepee, the boy told Long Arrow that if he could catch a glimpse of the old man's feet, then he could ask for a gift. Some days later, Long Arrow managed to see the feet of the old man, which were not really feet at all but hooves like those of the Elk Dog. When he realized that Long Arrow had seen his feet, the old man granted him three wishes. Long Arrow asked for the old man's multicolored belt, his black medicine robe, and his Elk Dogs.

The old man gave him all he asked for, including half of his herd of Elk Dogs. The old man also told him that the belt and the robe had special powers: the robe would help him to sneak up on and catch the Elk Dogs, while the belt would reveal their songs and prayers, so Long Arrow could learn more about their nature. The old man also gave Long Arrow a magic rope, with which he could always catch any Elk Dog he wanted. Long Arrow returned to his village with the Elk Dogs, finally a hero.

Long Arrow certainly deserved the honor, for the horse made just about every aspect of Blackfeet life easier and more productive. Indeed, the horse bettered the lives of all the Plains tribes, who took to life with the horse as if they had been born to it. The introduction of the horse drastically increased the success of Blackfeet buffalo hunts. Blackfeet scouts could cover a much larger area in their search for bison, and Blackfeet hunters could easily travel long distances and reach distant herds.

Horses made the buffalo hunt itself easier and safer, although it remained dangerous—an average mature bull bison weighs about two thousand pounds, stands six feet tall at the chest, has two sharp, curved horns, and becomes even more dangerous when frightened or wounded. A hunting party on horses, armed with arrows and lances, could get close to a herd and surround a group of buffalo. When the frightened buffalos tried to flee, a few of the bravest hunters would drive their horses into the center of the fray, then each would ride up alongside a chosen buffalo and, using their lances, arrows, or later, guns, would puncture its diaphragm, heart, or lungs. Often a buffalo had to be struck several times before finally going down; a healthy bison could kill horses, gore hunters, and then run for a mile, all after being fatally wounded.

The Blackfeet could also pack and haul a much heavier load on the horses than they could on the dogs. A larger pack animal meant a family could have a larger tepee and more possessions. The Blackfeet also made a cagelike structure from bentwood and mounted it atop the travois so that the horses could carry children. This made their migrations much faster, which in turn made it much easier for them to follow the bison herds or escape from enemies or natural disasters.

The horse changed Blackfeet society as well. Well-trained horses that could quietly approach prey or an enemy, could maintain a gallop for long distances, and would remain calm in battle and in the hunt were extremely valuable. As a result, wealth began to be determined by the number of horses one owned, and horses began to be used as dowries or bride-prices. If a brave gave a few of his finest horses to a visitor, it was an impressive gesture of great wealth, akin to burning currency or leaving a $100 tip in contemporary American culture. Wealthy

Porcupine quilled pipe and stem, bag of kinnikinnick (a combination of tobacco and herbs), and cutting board, Provincial Museum, Edmonton, Alberta. The Blackfeet used pipes like this one to smoke tobacco, which played a large part in many of their religious ceremonies and was the only crop the tribe grew.

Grizzly bear claw necklace, Provincial Museum, Edmonton, Alberta. Bears were revered by the Blackfeet for their perceived ability to heal themselves when wounded, and the Blackfeet proudly wore these ornamental necklaces.

Parfleche, Provincial Museum, Edmonton, Alberta. Many Plains tribes, including the Blackfeet, used these rawhide carrying cases to transport domestic goods and dried food.

D

Shield, club, and dagger, Provincial Museum, Edmonton, Alberta. Shields were often painted by the Blackfeet before they went off to battle to ensure good fortune and to protect themselves.

A hide saddle bag, beaded and fringed, from the Blood people, Provincial Museum, Edmonton, Alberta.

Weasel tail shirt, Provincial Museum, Edmonton, Alberta. The Blackfeet used buffalo hides that were tanned and made into shirts, robes, leggings, coats, dresses, and moccasins, among other forms of clothing.

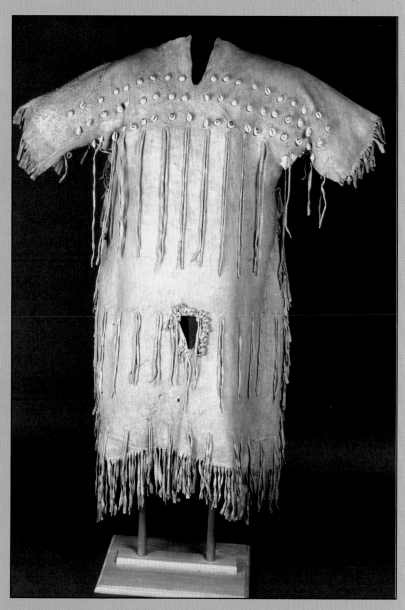

Hide dress with the bodice decorated with cowrie shells, Provincial Museum, Edmonton, Alberta.

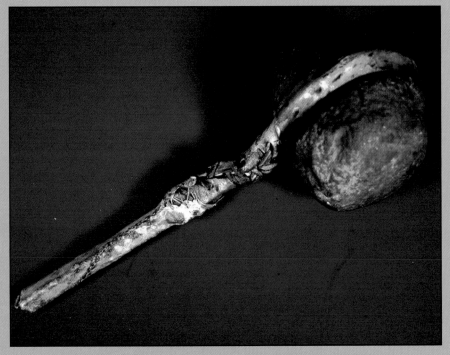

Stone head maul, Provincial Museum, Edmonton, Alberta. This wooden-headed hammer was used by the Blackfeet to split wood.

Blackfeet by definition owned many horses, while poor Blackfeet owned few or none and often had to borrow horses in order to hunt.

A horse became the brave's most valued hunting companion and was often painted to match the body or facial paint of its owner. A horse that hunted well with his master was revered and cared for even more than the man's wife or wives—after all, a good hunting horse ensured a good supply of meat for the family, and the more meat a hunter could bring home, the more wives he could support. If it was rumored that horse thieves were around, a warrior's buffalo-hunting horse would sleep in the tepee with its master, while the warrior's wife or wives slept outside. Horses that were killed in service to their master were often memorialized in carvings or paintings.

Horses were believed to have souls that lived on after death and horses who survived fierce battles or seemingly mortal wounds were believed to have strong supernatural powers. There was even a horse cult that was founded by a man who had been shown dances and medicine in a dream by two of his horses; cult members were believed to be able to heal both people and horses, to alter the weather, and to influence the movements of the buffalo. Dying Blackfeet could request to have their favorite horses sacrificed after their death so that their spirit would have reliable mounts in the afterworld. The horses to be sacrificed would be painted with scenes depicting their owner's exploits, and then shot in the head at close range near their owner's grave, releasing the horse's spirit near the place of their owner's spirit. (The resulting body could be disposed of in any manner and did not interfere with the owner's body.) A poorer family might "sacrifice" the horse by simply clipping his mane and tail, just as a mourning wife might cut off all her hair. The horse was then recognized as being in mourning for its owner (although it was not allowed any respite from work).

Perhaps the most important effect of the horse from a historical standpoint was the way it massively increased the military power of the Blackfeet, enabling them to make frequent, lightning-quick raids on other tribes (albeit they were now subject to such raids themselves). The Blackfeet could go to war against more tribes and tribes that were quite far away. Elderly Blackfeet interviewed in the late nineteenth and early twentieth centuries recalled being at war with eight or nine tribes at a time, and mounted warriors regularly crossed the Rocky Mountains to the west and traveled as far south as Utah to attack enemy tribes. Horses not only increased the Blackfeet's military might, they made war all but inevitable. Horse raids against another tribe were viewed as tantamount to a declaration of war, and according to *anthropologist* and historian John C. Ewers: "the horse raid offered young men of poor parents their best opportunity for economic security and social advancement." Consequently, many attempts at peace negotiations (generally made by older chiefs who were already wealthy) failed due to horse raids made by younger men who were trying to establish themselves.

Although horses had a major impact on Blackfeet culture, their influence was a reflection of the singular importance of the buffalo to the survival of the Blackfeet. The buffalo remained not only the primary means of livelihood but the very foundation and symbol of Blackfeet society. As long as the buffalo was populous and free to roam the plains, the Blackfeet could be assured of their own prosperity and freedom.

# 3

# The Life of the Blackfeet

Given the pivotal role of the horse and buffalo in Blackfeet society, it is not surprising that hunting, horseback riding, and fighting skills were considered essential. Consequently, boys were taught rudimentary hunting skills at a young age and played hunting games with their peers that involved stalking each other and dodging lances and arrows. Later, they were taught more sophisticated skills by their elders such as how to track game, how to be brave, how to endure physical pain and hardship, and how to be alert to signs from both the physical and the spiritual worlds. To help them develop these skills, older boys and young men were encouraged to sit in on the conversations of their elders in order to listen and to learn. Girls' education also began early in life, but instead of being trained as hunters, they were trained in their important role as preparers of food and clothing. They learned how to sew moccasins, how to do

One of the most important rites of passage for both Blackfeet men and women was the vision quest, which marked the transition into adult life. The goal of the vision quest was to free one's mind and spirit from physical concerns; the seeker would abstain from water, food, and shelter in the hope of receiving a vision that would guide his/her life.

embroidery and beadwork, how to cook, and most importantly, how to dress game and tan hides.

Young men went through a number of ceremonies marking the various stages of their development in their effort to become both a hunter and a warrior. One of the most important was the vision quest, a rite of passage that marked the end of their childhood and the beginning of life as an adult. A young man would first meet with a special council of elders, who would advise him on how to go about his vision quest. Then, the candidate would undergo purification by fasting, a sweat lodge ritual, and bathing, all of which were surrounded with prayers and the burning of sweet herbs. The council of elders would then perform a ceremonial dance to ensure protection for the young man while he was alone in the wilderness.

The young man then left the tribe and found a special place relatively far from the tribe's camp where he would be alone. In order to free his mind and spirit from physical concerns, he would go without food, water, or shelter from the elements. During this time, usually four days in duration, he hoped to see a vision that would provide him with his own personal medicine. A vision might be the sighting of a bear, the hearing of words whispered on the wind, or the sighting of a strange flash of light in the night sky. Whatever vision the young man experienced would become his symbol and part of his personal medicine throughout the whole of his life. Although women did not go to lonely mountaintops as men did, they did pursue their own version of the vision quest, and their visions were taken just as seriously as those of the men. A woman would purify herself in the sweat lodge, usually with the help of several other women, and then would go alone to a nearby valley or a small hill in search of a vision.

Young men who were about to become warriors had a special role in the annual *Sun Dance* ceremony. The Sun Dance ceremony was a lengthy, ornate affair that was considered the highest form of thanksgiving and sacrifice, in which the entire tribe would participate. It was generally performed in the late spring or early summer during a full moon and was sponsored by a different woman each year. Usually the sponsor was a woman of high standing in the tribe who, earlier in the year, had asked the sun to grant her a favor. If the favor had been granted, the woman sponsored the Sun Dance to repay the sun. The sponsor became the Sacred Woman of the Dance and had to fast for days before the ceremony. During the dance, the Sacred Woman would wear a special Sun Dance headdress, a robe of elk skin, and a dress of antelope and deer skins, and she would be treated with deep respect throughout the ceremony by everyone in the tribe. The Sacred Woman would also give away a number of horses during the ceremony, making the dance an expensive one to sponsor.

The ceremony would begin with a plea to the Sun God for the recovery of the sick, which was followed by a period when the entire tribe would fast and pray for their healing. Established warriors would fast and wound themselves as a sacrifice to the sun in repayment for the times they had been rescued from danger. After the fasting and the self-mutilation of the older warriors, the tribe would join together in feasting and joyous celebration, wearing their best clothes, riding the horses of which they were most proud, and asking special favors of the Creator.

For young warriors-to-be, the Sun Dance was a time to prove their courage. These men would first gather branches to build a frame for a sweat lodge—a ritual in itself, with the branch bearers first singing and dancing around the tepee of a medicine woman. Then they would purify themselves in the sweat lodge, while older warriors stood in a specially erected Sun Dance Lodge and told stories of their exploits. This was followed by a period of fasting and purification, after which the young men, ceremonially painted and prepared by their Sun Dance sponsors, would enter the Sun Dance Lodge to begin the actual Sun Dance. They would wear necklaces made of bone beads on a band of hide or beaded necklaces with weasel skin hanging from them. They also wore a special cloth, which hung from the waist to the ankles, and, according to some accounts, had sage wreaths on their heads.

The dance itself was extremely painful; withstanding it without fainting was a sign of excellent physical endurance. One person at a time performed the dance. The dancers' chest or back skin was pierced with a wooden skewer and attached to a hide thong; the thong, in turn, was attached by a rope to the center lodge pole. The dancers would swing, dancing on their toes, pulling against the thongs of the skewers. While dancing, they would focus their attention and energy on a sacred medicine bundle tied at the top of the lodge pole and would blow whistles made from eagle bone, the sound of which they believed would be heard by the Great Spirit. Any visions that came to a dancer during this ordeal were considered especially holy and meaningful. The dancer was accompanied by a helper, who aided him in preparing for the dance and gave him encouragement during the dance. Sometimes a young woman would be allowed to give the dancer a bit of chewed herb to renew his strength. Because of the body weight pulling on the skewer, it would eventually rip free from the flesh, ending the dance. The flesh torn from the dancers' bodies was left at the base of the center lodge pole as an offering to the sun.

After the Sun Dance, people were encouraged to give gifts to the poor, and sometimes chiefs gave new names to warriors who had outdone themselves in battle. New chiefs were appointed if replacements were necessary. The entire Sun Dance ceremony lasted about ten days.

Once a man had been to war or taken part in a successful horse raid, he was considered a warrior and worthy of a wife. When a man wished to marry, he would have a friend or relative bring a gift of horses to the lodge of the prospective bride's family. If the woman accepted the proposal, she would feed or water the horses or let them mingle with her father's herd. If she rejected the suitor, she either ignored the horses or had them returned to him. Sometimes marriages were arranged, and in any case the prospective groom usually knew what the woman's response would be, so the giving and receiving of horses often were simply a formal token of the engagement. The wedding would take place soon after the woman accepted the horses, usually within a few days. The bride left her family's

The Sun Dance was the most important yearly ceremony for many Plains tribes, including the Blackfeet. The ceremony, traditionally held in mid-summer, served as a spiritual renewal for both the participants and their relatives, as well as a renewal for life on Earth. Shown here is a young man performing the Sun Dance on the Piegan Reservation in Montana, during the 1890s.

tepee and came into her husband's lodge, accompanied by gifts, personal possessions, and horses that equaled or exceeded the groom's in value. Some accounts maintain that the marriage was formalized by the cutting and uniting of the couple's fingers, so their blood would mingle, symbolizing that they were now one flesh. There was always a big feast after the wedding.

In addition to the large, ornate religious ceremonies that marked important phases in a person's life, smaller ceremonies surrounded everyday activities such as eating, smoking, and hunting. The Blackfeet felt that the flora and fauna surrounding them had spiritual powers and shared a sort of kinship with humans, because all living things were made by the same creator.

This respect for things from the earth extended to the animals they killed for food and even the roots and berries they ate and used in their food and medicine. Consequently, religious ceremonies were not relegated to one day of the week but occurred continually throughout each day to honor and appease the spirits of the living things used. These ceremonies had to be faithfully and exactly executed to ensure success (especially during the preparation of hazardous undertakings such as a battle or a hunt), otherwise the spirits would be displeased, and the entire tribe could suffer as a result.

Not surprisingly, many animals in addition to the buffalo had places of importance in Blackfeet religion. Bears were revered because they were believed to have the ability to heal themselves when wounded and were invulnerable to other animals' attacks. Wolves were considered highly intelligent; consequently, reconnaissance scouts in a war party wore wolf skins as special medicine. The butterfly was thought to bring sleep; a mother would sew a piece of hide to resemble a butterfly and tie it in her infant's hair at night to ensure a good night's rest, and tepees were sometimes painted with a butterfly symbol in order to bring on powerful dreams.

Nonliving things also contained spiritual importance. The wind was considered a special messenger of the creator, who would send words of wisdom to the people through it. The circle was believed to best represent the life cycle; consequently, tepees had circular bases, and ceremonial dances followed a circular path (usually in a clockwise direction). The six directions—sky, earth, north, south, east, and west—were believed to have various attributes, and the most revered of these directions was the east, which was the place of the rising sun and thus the place of the origin of life.

One means of honoring the diverse powers inhabiting the Blackfeet spiritual world was through smoking pipes filled with *kinnikinnick,* a mixture of various dried barks, herbs, and tobacco. Smoking was done to protect the smoker from evil,

## Tobacco:
### The "Sacred Weed"

Blackfeet and other Native American nations have cultivated and prized tobacco for use in praying and for pleasure. Blackfeet people believed the smoke from burning tobacco was the breath of the Great Spirit, and that the people's prayers went to heaven along with the smoke.

Much in keeping with the myths and legends of the origin of the People and of the earth, tobacco's origin myth goes something like this: Long ago there were four brothers, all wise and spiritual men. Two of the brothers each had a vision, in which a voice showed them where to find the first tobacco plant. The third brother had a vision in which a voice showed him how to make a pipe by hollowing out a bone. The fourth brother also had a vision, this one showing him how to smoke the sacred weed. When they shared the pipe, the brothers felt clear-minded and all-powerful. Instead of sharing *nawak'osis* with the rest of the people as they had been instructed to do in their visions, the brothers kept the tobacco hidden and guarded.

There was much dissent among the people then, for they all knew that the four brothers were keeping something special from them. Eventually one young warrior named Bull-By-Himself and his wife set out to discover where the *nawak'osis* was planted.

They encamped alone in their tepee near the shores of a lake, and there the wife befriended four beavers. The beavers said they would lead the young warrior to the sacred weed if he would agree to spare their lives when hunting-time came. The young warrior agreed.

The beavers gathered the seeds from the growing *nawak'osis* and gave it to the man and his wife, instructing them how to plant the seeds and giving them the sacred songs to sing as they did so. When the four brothers discovered this, they thought, "No one knows about *nawak'osis* but us. They aren't planting our sacred weed. Only we have it." Then when it was nearly harvesttime, a hail storm came, destroying the four brothers' tobacco crop but sparing the warrior's crop. The man and his wife gladly shared their tobacco harvest with the people, and it has been that way ever since.

In keeping with the tradition of regarding tobacco as a sacred gift, there are many specialty shops and catalogs offering "native-grown" tobacco and native-made smoking implements.

Renowned frontier photographer Edward Curtis took this photo of two Blackfeet men inside a Piegan Lodge in 1910. In the lower center of the photo is a pipe and tobacco cutting board. Tobacco was the only crop the Blackfeet grew and it was known as the "sacred weed" for the important role it played in religious ceremonies.

attract game, invoke a spiritual blessing, or seal a pact. A special pipe called a *calumet*, or peace pipe, was smoked at the agreement of treaties and was carried by messengers of peace from one tribe to another. Special medicine pipes, which were used to cure sickness or to bring peace and prosperity to the tribe, were also called Thunder's Pipes, because it was believed that Thunder had given the pipe to humanity. Pipes were decorated in elaborate ways and always treated with great reverence. Eagle feathers were used to decorate pipes because eagles flew very high and very close to the life-giving sun and were consequently believed to be a mediator between the people and Creator Sun. Sometimes the entire eagle was used to wrap the pipe to give it extra power.

The tobacco smoked in the pipes was the sole plant cultivated by the Blackfeet. Tobacco was viewed as a holy and magical plant, and its cultivation was part of a sacred ceremony, surrounded by elaborate taboos, rituals, and beliefs. Tobacco seeds were planted when all the bands of a particular division camped together, then were abandoned but not forgotten when the bands split up. The division would reunite in the area when the tobacco was ready to harvest (the plants were supposedly tended by magical beings in the meantime), and the harvest would be distributed among band members.

Symbols were believed to have a very real power to protect and aid a person; consequently, the designs that covered Blackfeet clothes, faces, bodies, and armaments almost always contained significant symbolic value. Men's painted bodies often reflected their accomplishments in war or the hunt; for example, if a warrior killed an enemy in hand-to-hand combat, he might paint a hand on each of his shoulders to symbolize his victory. Before going out to hunt or fight, men would often paint protective symbols or scenes outlining a successful expedition on their bodies. After a victorious battle, Blackfeet warriors painted their faces black to indicate their success. Painting the face and body had practical as well as symbolic use, and everybody wore some form of paint everyday, most commonly painting their faces red. In the summertime, the paint served as a sunscreen, while in cold weather, the paint protected the skin from the cold and from chapping. (Much of the protection against the cold came from the layer of bear or buffalo grease that the Blackfeet applied to the skin when preparing it for painting.)

Shields carried into battle were often adorned with the image of an animal that had come to the shield's owner during a vision quest. If, for example, a man had envisioned a turtle during his vision quest, then it was believed that the spirit of the turtle would look after and protect that man. Consequently, he would paint a turtle shell on his shield to

ensure good fortune in battle. War bonnets were also frequently decorated with the fur or feathers of animals that had
appeared in the wearer's visions. Certain *talismans* would help
the hunter or warrior even if the animal represented had not
been a part of his personal vision quest, and experienced
hunters often gave useful talismans to younger men. One common talisman was made out of a stuffed kingfisher; because the
bird symbolized agility and speed, warriors believed this charm
would help them avoid enemy arrows.

Lodges were also painted with symbols. Often, the base was
painted red to symbolize the earth, and within this red there
would be unpainted orbs to represent stars. Next, the lodge
painter would add hills or peaks, with the top of the lodge
painted black to symbolize the sky at night. Tepees were often
painted with geometric borders on the top and bottom and
then decorated with designs, which told of the exploits of the
tepee's owner. A Blackfeet warrior with an exceptionally illus-
trious record would paint his tepee liner with pictographs com-
memorating his accomplishments.

The adornment of clothing was considered so important
that the maker would often seek a vision or some other sort of
sign from the spirit world for inspiration. Men's clothing was
decorated with symbols of prowess in the hunt or in battle,
while women's clothing—which was not permitted to bear
realistic scenes—was decorated with geometric designs. Most
clothing was made from buffalo hide (although in the late eighteenth century, when trade began with the Hudson's Bay
Trading Company, clothes were sometimes made from the
company's colorful blankets) and was decorated with porcupine quills and corn husks that were colored with vegetable
dyes and sewn onto the hide. Fringes were made by cutting
extra hide at the seams into strips, and pendants, sometimes
made from deer toes, were hung onto the clothing.

For special occasions, such as important religious ceremonies, men would wear shirts made from bighorn sheepskin,

which was soft and white. These shirts were so ornately decorated that they could not be washed and were simply painted brown or red when dirty. War shirts were also made of special hide, usually deer or antelope, and had full sleeves with a fringe of some skins hanging from them. Not only did specific outfits have meaning, but the way in which clothing was worn indicated a certain feeling or intent. A young man courting a bride would wear his buffalo robe over his head, while an older man carried one end of the robe in his left arm, with his right arm unencumbered. During ceremonies, women covered their heads with their robes.

The Blackfeet also made hats from fur or bird skin for use in cold weather. In addition to this practical headwear, fancy headdresses were worn during special events. During victory parties or warrior society meetings, Blackfeet men wore full feather headdresses. Blackfeet women also wore headdresses during special occasions, most notably the Sun Dance, when the Sacred Woman of the Dance wore a headdress made of a headband adorned with beads, quills, and feathers and having two long feathers pointing up on either side and a dozen or so animal tails hanging down from it. The sponsor had to buy this expensive headdress from the previous Sacred Woman of the Dance and keep it until the next Sun Dance.

Unlike some other Plains tribes, the Blackfeet usually grew their hair long. Both men and women washed and brushed their hair often and waxed it with buffalo fat to make it shine, but while Blackfeet women simply parted their hair and wore it in long braids, Blackfeet men had much more ornate hairstyles. Men wore bangs and adorned their hair with feathers or quills, while medicine men sometimes coiled their hair around their forehead so that it stuck out like a horn; this unusual hairstyle indicated their position within the tribe.

In addition to clothing and headwear, animal products were used to make tools and decorations. A porcupine's tail made a fine hairbrush, and its quills were used as paintbrush handles, as well as ornamentation for clothing. Bear, otter, deer (especially does), coyote, lynx, and wolf were prized for their fur and skin, and their hides were used in clothing, weapon, and tepee ornamentation and the making of drums or headdresses. Elk antlers were used as bows to play fiddle-like musical instruments, with horsehair being used for the strings. The more northern Blackfeet hunted moose, while those located higher in the Rocky Mountains hunted wild sheep and mountain goats for food, clothing, and tools. Beaver pelts became a valuable trade commodity as European traders began to infiltrate Blackfeet territory; as a result, the beaver was hunted to the brink of extinction by whites and Native Americans alike. Later, similar overhunting was to occur with the buffalo.

Not all tools came from animals; stones were frequently used as weapons and as mortars and pestles used for making pemmican. Hot stones were used in cooking dishes such as stews. Most food was cooked inside a cooking bag made from the stomach lining of a large animal such as a buffalo, which could not be directly exposed to fire; heated stones would be placed in the stew itself in order to cook the dish. Heated stones were also placed in sweat lodges, where water would be poured over them to create steam. Wood also had a great variety of uses: wooden sticks were used as stirrers during the preparation of meals, as pegs for piercing and stretching hides, and as frames for tepees, travois, sweat lodges, and *bull boats* (bowl-shaped vessels made of hide over a wooden frame that were used to ferry people and supplies across rivers). Wood was also used for cradle-boards and was bent into the cage-like structure that was placed on a travois in order to transport children. Stout tree limbs were carved to make the handle for a *quirt*, which was a combination wooden war club and rawhide horse-whip. Grasses, reeds, and vines were made into baskets for carrying babies and supplies.

The staple of the Blackfeet diet was buffalo meat. After a hunt, the women would roast large pieces of meat on skewers hung over the flame from a tripod. Small bits of meat were cooked in a pot with wild roots and vegetables to make stew. Intestines were cleaned out and stuffed with a mixture of meat and wild sage and onion, making a kind of sausage. Bones that could not be used for other purposes would be broken and added to stew to make use of their marrow.

The Blackfeet varied their buffalo meat diet with other animals, such as deer, antelope, quail, and rabbit—but not fish, which for reasons unknown was taboo. The women supplemented the meat by gathering and preparing wild herbs, such as sage; vegetables, such as wild peas and prairie turnips; and wild fruits, such as berries, persimmons, and chokecherries. Prickly-pear cactus, milkweed buds, and rosehips were used in buffalo stew. Other vegetables were obtained by trade with the Mandans and Pawnees, who cultivated and sold beans, corn, squash, and pumpkins. Blackfeet women could preserve food for times of famine by making pemmican or by making a *cache*, which was a stash of food buried in a large hole in the ground.

The Blackfeet lived well off their land, efficiently utilizing the natural resources available. Their nomadic existence, considered "backward" by white observers, was well suited to the climate and conditions of the northern Great Plains. Likewise, their social and political organization was suited to their nomadic condition and enabled the Blackfeet to flourish on the harsh plains, and, not incidentally, to become an important military power in the area.

# 4

# The Social Structure of the Blackfeet

One notable element of Blackfeet society—in stark contrast to the norm in Europe and even in the United States of the eighteenth and nineteenth centuries—was the flexibility of rank in the tribe. Any man, regardless of birth, could attain a high social rank, provided he lived according to the spoken and unspoken laws and spiritual guidelines that governed the tribe. In addition, a man could govern only with the consent of the people over whom he presided for as long as was thought fit. For example, a chief usually simply retired around age forty, when his physical prowess began to wane; he did not have to be forced out or overthrown. A new chief would then be chosen by consensus.

The structure of divisions and bands within the tribe was similarly flexible. Although the three divisions within the tribe remained the same, the divisions were linguistically and culturally identical, engaged in frequent friendly interaction, and were close allies during any hostilities. Each division was made up of several bands, which were groups of individuals that varied in size. Band structure was extremely loose; although a person usually belonged to their father's or husband's band, this was not always the case, and a person could leave one band and join another at will. Indeed, band members were frequently not related by blood, and although the Blackfeet had a strong incest taboo, marriage within a band was permitted. The bands usually grouped together according to their division during activities such as the Sun Dance or the buffalo hunts, but at other times each band would go its own way to hunt and travel.

The Blackfeet were not governed by one chief, but instead different bands were each overseen by their own chiefs. Sometimes a council of chiefs would gather for important decisions, such as when considering a *treaty*, but no chief was officially more powerful than another and a chief who did not agree with a decision was free to ignore it. New bands could be formed at any time; a man with sufficient standing to become a chief would sometimes simply move away from his old band, and whoever followed him became part of the new band. To attract followers, a would-be chief needed to be a leader in war, in the hunt, and in religious life; in addition, he had to be a charitable and generous man. These characteristics were considered important because it was believed that the nature of the band followed the temperament of the chief. If he was just, calm, and wise, so were his people; if he was not, his band would cause trouble.

Blackfeet bands had *war chiefs*, who planned battle strategy and led warriors during times of war, and *peace chiefs*, who settled disputes and set policy during times of peace. Peace chiefs also kept a yearly record of events called the Winter Count. Each year, an event that affected the band as a whole would be recorded, or if no major event had occurred, a remarkable personal event would be recorded instead. Sometimes the Winter Count was kept in pictographs painted on hides, but most commonly it was a verbal record that was memorized by the chief. A few of these were recorded by historians in the late nineteenth and early twentieth century, and when compared against written records of the same period, have demonstrated a remarkable accuracy.

Despite the chief's role as leader, the judicial system under which the Blackfeet lived was usually administered by someone other than the chief. This judge would direct or approve a punishment, which was then meted out by a special council or by relatives of either the wronged or the wrongdoer. Loyalty to the tribe and tribe members was considered tantamount; the punishment for anyone accused of disloyalty to the tribe was death on sight. Crimes against other people were punished severely; someone who murdered another tribe member could be punished by death, and a woman who committed adultery could have her nose cut off. Crimes against property, however, were treated more leniently; in cases of theft, the stolen property was simply returned to its rightful owner.

Order was kept with the aid of the Blackfeet warrior societies. These societies punished offenders, protected the tribe, and presided over organized raids and hunts. The societies were only open to men, and most of them only accepted members from a certain age group. For example, young men who had gone on a vision quest and had participated in a horse raid joined the Doves, while warrior candidates were members of the Mosquitoes until they had proved themselves in battle, at which time they could join the Braves. Generally speaking, societies made up of older, more experienced warriors were more venerated and respected; these included the Bulls and the Brave Dogs.

Other types of societies also existed, with various functions and requirements for membership. Police societies were temporary societies that drew their members, usually younger men who still had to prove themselves, from the warrior societies. They were organized for special functions where a number of

Each Blackfeet tribe—the Piegan, the Blood, and the Siksika—had their own societies, which practiced their own unique dances, songs, and ceremonies. Shown here are members of the Matoki women's society (Blood) erecting a ceremonial lodge.

rival bands would be present, and they helped to keep the peace. Religious societies had tightly restricted memberships and performed serious ceremonies, such as the secret, sacred rituals performed during the Sun Dance ceremony by the members of the Horn Society. Their activities were held in conjunction with the only women's society, the Buffalo Bull Society; both societies were so prestigious that they had their own lodges for special religious rites during the Sun Dance ceremony. Unlike religious societies, dance societies, such as the Kisapas, or Hair Parters, were loosely organized and more social in nature. For example, when the Kisapas held their special dance, participation was open to any young man with the appropriate costume, and their dance served mainly to celebrate and honor the generosity, bravery, and military skill of deserving men.

Warriors could move into a more prestigious society by gaining honor in battle. Honor could be gained by undertaking a dangerous activity known as *counting coup*. The more dangerous an activity was, the more honor was gained by its successful completion. Consequently, killing an enemy in an ambush did not gain a warrior any status, but taking the gun of a living enemy was extremely prestigious. A common form of counting coup was to touch a living or recently killed enemy with a lance, a hand, or a special stick called a coup stick. The enemy was not harmed in the process (although he was usually already wounded), and the more heavily armed and dangerous an enemy was, the greater the regard for the warrior who successfully counted coup against him. Warriors would recount their coups with scrupulous accuracy during the Sun Dance and other gatherings of warriors; a man who exaggerated his exploits was considered inveterately dishonest and crafty.

Men who were of a more spiritual bent than the warriors could become shamans, or holy men, providing fellow tribespeople with physical and spiritual healing. Shamans could never charge for their services, but it was customary for them to receive gifts of gratitude from the families of healed patients. Although white settlers tended to lump together any Native American they saw involved in healing or religious rituals under the general term "medicine man," there were actually distinct categories of practitioners among the shamans.

Certain Blackfeet acted as physicians, and these physicians further specialized by treating different illnesses. Every person in the tribe had their own medicine bundle, a collection of items that provided protection for the owner. In the event of an illness or injury, the sick person could meditate on their bundle, but if the condition did not improve, a physician was summoned. The physician used many tools to aid in the victim's recovery, and although each physician had their own methods, they often used herbs, incantations, hot baths, dancing, and the shaking of medicine rattles over the sick person's body.

Physicians were constantly on the lookout for new healing herbs, discovering them through visions or by observing activities of animals (especially bears, who were believed to have a special ability to find useful plants). After learning of a plant with special curative powers, the doctors then experimented on themselves or on patients to determine its proper usage. Sometimes they or their patients died as a result of such trial and error, but the medicine used by the Plains Indians in general was skillfully administered and often successful. Indeed,

## What's Old Is New Again

Innovations continue to be made in the field of science and more specifically in medicine. And upon taking a second look, it would seem that history is repeating itself. For example, there has been a growing trend in recent decades in the use of historically helpful herbs, and scientists are now also pointing out the healing and medicinal qualities of foods people such as the Blackfeet ate for centuries as part of their daily diet. Blueberries, for example, are rich in antioxidants, while squash is high in fiber and Vitamin C. In the herb world, plants and roots have been used for ages to treat illnesses and pains of all kinds. The well-known willow bark has proven historically useful as a pain reliever. Now modern people know that willow—with its active ingredient of salicylic acid, also known as aspirin—can ease aches, pains, fevers, and even offset a heart attack.

Some of the latest findings in the scientific world also confirm what Blackfeet people have known since time began: that sounds can be useful in healing the body and spirit. Recently, scientists tested brain waves of people who listened to ceremonial drum-beats. The scientists discovered that their subjects' brains' alpha waves increased after listening to the beats, inducing clarity of thought and calmness of mood and emotion. Even the subjects' heart rates showed reduced signs of stress.

It seems that in moving forward into "modern" times, contemporary mainstream society is discovering cures found by looking backward in history and the wisdom of the natural world.

many medicines used today were originally used by Native American healers.

Blackfeet doctors dressed simply, but they were easily identified by their unique headdresses. These headdresses were made out of buffalo horn, had hair on the front that was dyed in several colors, and had a fur-like tail hanging down the back with feathers and beaded disks dangling on its end. In addition to healing people, Blackfeet doctors treated the tribe's animals and also gave charms to warriors before battle to ensure success. Some doctors also made love bundles, which could be worn by a person desiring another's affections as a type of love potion.

If a doctor could not help a patient, a priest or holy man was sent for. If a sick tribal member was in grave danger, the holy man would sometimes have all the tribespeople gather in a circle around the dying one. They would pray, and the holy man would dance, sing, shake rattles holding special medicine, and make the sounds of the animals that he believed would aid him most in an attempt to revive the patient.

Holy men were not only healers or priests; they were prophets who had a much deeper connection with and knowledge of the spiritual world than doctors or ordinary tribespeople. Holy men dressed much more elaborately than doctors, and much of what they did is shrouded in mystery. White people were seldom allowed to view ceremonies involving a holy man, and after one's death, his costumes, which held his personal medicine, were usually burned. Holy men were able to predict important things such as the location of buffalo, the outcome of a battle or raid, and the approach of danger. They conducted rituals to help solve any number of problems, including finding missing children.

While Blackfeet men acted primarily as warriors, hunters, and to a lesser extent, shamans, women were the primary caretakers of the tribe. They provided and prepared food, clothing, and shelter for the family; bore and reared children; and made sure camp moves came off quickly and successfully. These duties were not seen as drudgery; on the contrary, they were essential for the tribe's survival and Blackfeet women took pride in their skills in these fields. Women who were exceptionally talented in beadwork, quillwork, or painting could attain high status within the tribe.

Because of the high fatality rate among Blackfeet men, women provided continuity for the tribe. Consequently, they were protected during camp moves by being placed behind the men, who would have to face any dangers first (a tradition misconstrued by European observers as a gesture of disdain). The high proportion of women in the tribe contributed to the popularity of polygamy, which became even more common as the introduction of the horse increased the number of wives a warrior could support. Although polygamy was viewed as disrespectful or sinful by European observers, it was considered desirable by women as well as men because a family unit with more than one wife could prepare much more food. One woman working alone could dress only eight or ten buffalo during a year's time, while six or more working together could dress more than one hundred. Indeed, first wives sometimes asked their husbands to bring another wife into the tepee in order to help her with the work. Often successive wives were sisters of the first, ensuring cooperation in the arduous task of dressing game.

The division of the genders among the Blackfeet was not a firm one. Men often made their own clothing, and older, married women with the appropriate gifts could become shamans. According to John Ewers, before the 1880s it was common for young, childless women to accompany their men in battle, hunting, or on raids. Although these women primarily performed such essential duties as cooking and maintaining the camp, they also participated fully in waging war and would help herd stolen horses back to their tribe.

If a woman showed talent in making war, riding a horse, or hunting, those skills were cultivated, and some Blackfeet

Gender lines were never rigid among the Blackfeet; men often made their own clothes and women often accompanied men into battle. Shown here is Weasel Tail, a Piegan warrior, whose wife, Throwing Down, fought alongside him during five battles, until the birth of their first child brought her career as a warrior to an end.

women became famous warriors and leaders of their tribes. One such woman was Elk Hollering in the Water, who was born around 1870 and who, after marriage, went with her husband, Bear Chief, on raids against enemy tribes. She won high regard for her successful raids, especially her horse raids. (It is important to note that stealing was only considered criminal when it occurred within one's own tribe; when a member of a raiding party took an enemy's possessions it was seen as a form of counting coup.) Another woman named Throwing Down fought at the side of her husband, Weasel Tail, for five battles, until the birth of their first child put an end to her career as a warrior. Throwing Down was reportedly very much in love with her husband and went into battle to protect him.

Sometimes a woman who had lost her husband or family members in a battle against an enemy tribe would be included in the next party to attack that tribe in order to obtain vengeance. One such woman was Pitamahkan, or Running Eagle, perhaps the most famous of all Blackfeet women warriors. Just after she married, her husband was killed in a fight against the Crows. Running Eagle prayed to the sun and asked for a way to avenge her husband's death. She was told in a dream to go on a vision quest, so she went to a cave hidden behind a waterfall then known as Trick Falls, near what is now known as Two Medicine Lodges near East Glacier, Montana.

There she had a vision in which the sun told her that if she became a warrior, she would be successful—but only as long as she remained true to her husband's memory. For years, Running Eagle led hunting, raiding, and warring missions. She could outshoot, outride, and outlast most of her male counterparts, and she was even admitted into the ordinarily all-male Brave Dogs Warrior Society. But in 1860, shortly after responding to the attentions of another Blackfeet warrior, Running Eagle was accosted by a camp guard during a reconnaissance mission into an enemy Flathead camp and was shot. To memorialize the young warrior, in 1981 the name of the waterfall where she had her vision quest was changed from Trick Falls to Running Eagle Falls.

Adventurous warriors and hunters like Running Eagle, who dashingly pursued glory and in the process provided their tribe with food, goods, and security, epitomized Blackfeet culture to many white observers. Although obviously many Blackfeet who were equally important to the survival of the tribe were not warriors, the warriors' lethal skills became increasingly important as their territory was slowly invaded by a strange new tribe, a group of men from the East who trapped beaver, shot buffalo, traded strange items, and called themselves Americans.

# 5

# Exposure to Other Worlds

The period between 1750 and 1850—that is, the approximate time between the introduction of the horse and the major influx of white settlers onto Blackfeet land—was one of great prosperity and comparative isolation for the Blackfeet. Although by the early seventeenth century Spanish explorers such as Francisco Vásquez de Coronado had traveled northward toward the Great Plains, their interactions with the Blackfeet were for the most part limited to being the victims of horse raids.

The first white person to have a more nuanced relation with the tribe also gave a firsthand account of the more ordinary interactions between the Europeans and the Blackfeet. David Thompson, an agent from a British trading company known as the North West Company (which later merged with Hudson's Bay Company), lived among a Piegan band in 1787 and witnessed the triumphant return of a raiding party with twelve mules and thirty horses. The party had

During the eighteenth and nineteenth centuries, the Blackfeet traded extensively with the Hudson's Bay Company, which controlled the area of present-day Alberta until it sold the future province to Canada in 1870. Shown here is a contemporary sketch of one of the company's nineteenth-century trading posts in Alberta.

set out to attack the Shoshonis but, unable to find the tribe, had pressed on for another 1,500 miles looking for a new target. They surprised a group of Spaniards with a long train of pack mules and horses, frightened away the men, and gleefully led the stock back to their camp.

The first American explorers to encounter the Blackfeet very nearly fell victim to horse raiders. Meriwether Lewis and William Clark spent the years 1804 through 1806 exploring the vast area obtained by President Thomas Jefferson in the Louisiana Purchase. During part of the expedition, Lewis and

Clark temporarily split up to explore different areas of the Rocky Mountains, and Lewis led a party of four men with horses and supplies up the Marias River. Lewis, who described the Blackfeet as "a strong and honest people," discovered their aggressive side as his party was attacked by eight Blackfeet horse raiders. The Lewis party managed to outfight the warriors, killing two of them and taking their horses and weapons, but they had to flee the area in fear of pursuit by vengeful Blackfeet warriors.

The 1800s saw an ever-increasing number of hostile encounters between the whites and the Blackfeet. Americans had avoided the Great Plains, which lacks the lush vegetation of the woodlands in the eastern United States and seemed a wasteland to trappers and settlers, who called the area the Great American Desert. But the whites' perception of the area would soon change. Shortly after Lewis and Clark returned to the eastern United States, they visited the city of St. Louis, Missouri, which at the time was home to a large number of fur trappers. Lewis and Clark's descriptions of an area teeming with game—especially the valuable beaver—fired the imaginations and ambitions of the fur trappers and freed the investment capital necessary to finance expeditions. Soon after Lewis and Clark's visit, a large number of trappers set off for the West.

An intense rivalry quickly developed between the Americans and the British who operated out of Canada. Trappers and traders attempted to ally themselves with the various tribes in the area in order to gain access to their land, and many were eventually befriended by tribes such as the Crow, Nez Perce, Flathead, Mandan, and Sioux. Because of their hostile encounter with Lewis, the Blackfeet remained suspicious of any overtures by whites. Their antagonism was inadvertently exacerbated by one of the first American trappers in the area, a man named John Colter.

Colter was an experienced woodsman who had traveled to the Rocky Mountains as part of the Lewis and Clark expedition, but left the expedition and remained in the unexplored and unsettled territory for the next six years, hoping to make his fortune in the fur trade. In 1808, he managed to convince the Crows and the Flatheads to send several hundred of their members with him to attend negotiations at a small, temporary trade outpost called Fort Manuel. Unfortunately, the Crows

## A Vastly Different Tail

The summer of 1806 was an eventful one for not only Lewis and Clark's Corps of Discovery but for the Plains Indians as a whole. While the aforementioned encounter in this book is based on details from the journal of Meriwether Lewis, Blackfeet tribal elders today recount a vastly different version of the initial meeting between American explorers and their own ancestors. In an interview in 2003, tribal elder G.G. Kipp related his ancestor's version of the story to the Blackfeet Community College Native American Scholars Program.

According to oral histories, Kipp said that Lewis and the rest of his group came upon some young Blackfeet boys from the small group known as the Skunk band. The boys were not "warriors" but were herding horses. The oral history says that the Corps of Discovery team spent the night encamped with the boys, competing in a footrace that evening in which the boys were victorious. In the morning, as the boys came to say good-bye and take their winnings, they were nearly all killed.

A similar story has been borne out by the "Father of Glacier National Park," George Bird Grinnell, who interviewed Chief Wolf Calf in 1895. At the time of the interview, Wolf Calf was 102 years old, but with clarity he was able to recount the story of when he witnessed the fight and subsequent murder of the young boys. Chief Wolf Calf accurately located the scene of the tragedy on a hill near Birch Creek, in Teton County.

While this explains why the Blackfeet closed their territory to whites for the next eighty years, a new attitude has emerged, and the Blackfeet people have supported the Lewis and Clark Bicentennial, which runs until 2006. They see the commemorations as an opportunity to celebrate their culture while also promoting tourism.

and the Flatheads were implacable enemies of the Blackfeet, who were not pleased with the notion of their rivals gaining access to more and better guns, horses, and supplies. Blackfeet warriors ambushed the Crow-Flathead contingency, and in order to retain the allies he had, Colter fought against the Blackfeet.

Colter was wounded in the battle, but upon his recovery he decided to try and gain the confidence of the Blackfeet. He entered their territory in the hopes of meeting peacefully with tribal leaders and making a trade agreement. Hoping to appear as unthreatening as possible, Colter took only one other person with him, a man named John Potts. Upon entering Blackfeet territory, Colter and Potts were promptly captured by a party of warriors—a turn of events that Colter met with aplomb, realizing that captivity might give him a good opportunity to meet chiefs who would be interested in trading with him. Potts, however, was less collected and tried to escape; when the warriors tried to stop him, he shot one and was immediately killed.

Any hope for a friendly alliance between the Blackfeet and American trappers died with Potts, and things looked grim for Colter as well when the vengeful warrior party decided to engage in a little sport. Stripping Colter naked, they set him loose and chased him on foot across the cactus-covered desert and rocky terrain. Colter proved to be swift, managing to outrun all but one warrior, who fell just as he was about to spear Colter. Thinking quickly, Colter dispatched the warrior with his own lance, hid himself under a pile of driftwood floating in a nearby river until the other warriors gave up the pursuit, and set out for Fort Manuel, three hundred miles away. He reached the fort only a week later—an impressive time, especially considering that he was without clothes, shoes, or supplies.

Colter's second encounter with the Blackfeet simply confirmed their belief that any whites in their territory were a threat. During the 1810s, while other tribes in the area took sides in the British-American struggle for land and power, the

Blackfeet attempted as much as possible to keep all whites out of their territory. A resurgence in the British and American fur trades during the 1820s resulted in a new push by trappers to open Blackfeet territory. In 1822, the Missouri Fur Company, which had been forced out of the Three Forks area by the Blackfeet some twelve years before, decided to try again. The company, along with a rival company established by trappers Andrew Henry and William Ashley, recruited hundreds of trappers wanting to reap the riches of the Rocky Mountains. The easiest way to travel into the mountains was to go up the various rivers that flowed from them, and the canoes and boats of the trappers soon formed a brisk river traffic.

But the Blackfeet were as stubborn and aggressive in 1823 as they had been in 1810—more than two dozen American trappers were killed and countless numbers were relieved of their supplies, guns, and furs by war parties. The Blackfeet were especially feared by the trappers both because they were consistently hostile to whites and because their raiding and hunting parties routinely traveled wide distances and never stayed in one clearly defined territory. (Indeed, in at least two cases the Blackfeet forced the abandonment of white settlements established deep within the territory of friendlier tribes.) The trappers quickly abandoned the dangerous river routes into the Rocky Mountains in favor of the less conspicuous overland routes, a decision that was to have egregious effects on all the Plains Indians when legendary mountain man Jedediah Smith led a party over South Pass, a gentle pass through the otherwise rugged Rocky Mountains that was large enough for covered wagons to use. Although it is probable that British explorers discovered the pass before the Smith party, they were the first to pass through it from east to west and to realize its value to settlers wishing to move to the Pacific Northwest. South Pass would eventually form an integral part of the Oregon Trail, the most popular travel route for the flood of settlers who moved west during the mid-nineteenth century.

Although land routes were somewhat safer than the rivers, neither were completely safe, and the fur trappers' insistence upon trespassing in Blackfeet territory led to vicious consequences. One fur trapper, Henry Vanderburgh, was ambushed, killed, and dismembered by Blackfeet warriors. In a grisly show of bravado, the warriors took Vanderburgh's limbs to Fort McKenzie and defiantly waved them to the soldiers within the walls. British traders also had strained relations with the Blackfeet, mainly because they traded with the hated Flatheads. But in the late 1820s, a former Hudson's Bay Trading Company trapper by the name of Jacob Berger was able to establish limited trade between the Blackfeet and the British traders. Eventually, overtrapping drove the beaver to the brink of extinction in the area, and by the 1830s, white fur trappers had mostly pulled out of Blackfeet territory.

Blackfeet hostility toward whites lessened somewhat with the departure of the trespassing trappers, and white travelers and traders who were not intent on exploiting Blackfeet land began to receive a warmer welcome. In the early 1830s, Arthur Philip Maximilian, natural historian and prince of Wied-Neuwied (in what is now Germany), explored the Great Plains region, witnessing Indian battles and camping and trapping with the Blackfeet. His meticulous notes on his experiences were published in London in 1843, along with the paintings of Carl Bodmer, an artist in Maximilian's entourage. Other artists also attempted to capture what they rightly viewed as a threatened way of life. Alfred Jacob Miller, a painter from Baltimore, was employed by Scottish mountaineer Sir William Stewart to travel with him and to paint what they saw. Miller's paintings of the Teton Sioux, the Wind River Mountains, and Chimney Rock have great emotional depth and achieved great popularity. But the artist who painted the most in-depth and objective depictions of nineteenth-century tribal life was George Catlin. From 1832 to 1840, Catlin traveled from the Great Lakes region to the Great Plains, visited more than forty tribes, including the

Blackfeet, and painted more than five hundred scenes depicting virtually every aspect of Native American life.

The 1840s saw the trickle of the white men into the West become a flood. During this period, endless streams of wagon trains filled with hundreds upon thousands of people both from the eastern United States and from foreign countries crossed the Great Plains in what became known as the Great Emigration. These settlers were primarily interested in settling the lands of the Pacific Northwest, but to get there they went along the Oregon Trail, overhunting the area, picking fights with Native American warriors, and permanently disrupting the migration patterns of the buffalo.

Most of this activity affected only the southern fringe of Blackfeet territory, but when gold was discovered in the Rocky Mountains in the 1850s, the situation changed drastically. Immediately, a huge influx of prospectors and settlers moved into Blackfeet territory, and a sharp increase in the number and severity of conflicts between the whites and the tribe followed the migration. The Americans promptly lobbied the U.S. government for protection against Native American raids, and the U.S. government responded with equal promptness, setting the borders of the Blackfeet Nation with the Treaty of Fort Laramie in 1851. The treaty was such only in the loosest sense of the word; the Blackfeet were not present, represented, or consulted during the treaty negotiations or signing. Not surprisingly, the treaty, which also allowed for roads and military outposts to be built on Blackfeet lands, proved impossible to enforce.

The first mutually recognized treaty between the U.S. government and the Blackfeet Indians was in 1855. Called Lamed Bull's Treaty (after a well-known chief of the same name), it stated that the U.S. government would pay the Blackfeet $20,000 per year in goods and services and devote $15,000 per year toward the "education and Christianization" of the Blackfeet. In return, the Blackfeet agreed to give up half their hunting area and to live in "perpetual peace" with their white neighbors, allowing whites to settle, travel, and build telegraphs, railroads, and missions in their territory.

Relations improved immediately following the signing of Lamed Bull's Treaty, as the Blackfeet helped white hunters bring down buffalo and traded the hides for wagons, beads, wool, and guns. Before long, however, whites began to abuse the treaty. The Blackfeet were given spoiled food, broken-down wagons, moth-eaten blankets, rusty guns, and an intoxicating liquid called alcohol that promptly caused a large number of fatalities.

An even more devastating trend in the nineteenth century was the near-elimination of the buffalo by white hunters. The "immence herds" of buffalo described by Lewis in his journal quickly dwindled in the first half of the nineteenth century as Europeans developed a taste for buffalo tongue and buffalo hide clothing became the new rage in European fashion. Native American hunting parties frequently discovered huge herds of dead bison with only their tongues and hides removed—a wasteful practice common to white hunters that appalled the Blackfeet. Even worse, after the transcontinental railroad was built in the 1860s, settlers in passing trains would shoot buffalo solely for sport, leaving the carcasses to rot on the plains. This sort of behavior seemed almost insane to the Blackfeet and increased their disdain for and belligerence toward whites.

The situation worsened in the 1860s when white settlers brought great herds of cattle to the former lands of the Blackfeet. These cattle competed with the native fauna for grass, and the practice of fencing off cattle interfered with the migration patterns of the buffalo. The near extermination of the buffalo was assured when in 1860 a German tannery came up with a way to make a refined grade of hide from buffalo skins and industrialists began to use the hide to make machinery belts. The price of hides skyrocketed, and the massacre of the buffalo reached a fever pitch as literally tens of thousands of white hunters swamped Blackfeet hunting lands. By 1883, only a handful of buffalo remained.

The Blackfeet did not placidly accept the reduction of their lands, the disappearance of the buffalo, and the duplicity of the whites. Retaliatory efforts, including attacks on small ranches and settlements, increased throughout the 1860s, and American vigilantes quickly returned in kind. Indeed, hostilities became so common that the Kainah division, which traditionally split its time between what are now Alberta and Montana, made the decision to remain in Canada on a permanent basis—as the Siksikas and some of the more northern bands of Piegans had already done. Finally, white settlers appealed to the *Bureau of Indian Affairs* (which at the time worked closely with the War Department) for redress.

On January 6, 1870, a detachment of U.S. Calvary, led by Colonel E.M. Baker, marched against a band of Piegans in an action known as the Piegan War. The band Baker chose as a target was completely unprepared for battle, having taken no part in raids against the whites and having been recently decimated by a severe smallpox epidemic. In addition, most of the warriors were away hunting, and the camp was primarily composed of elders, women, and children. Nonetheless, Baker ordered a surprise attack, and within minutes, his troops killed approximately two hundred Piegans with only one U.S. casualty (probably the result of friendly fire). The cruelty of the Baker Massacre (as the Piegan War soon was called) drew sharp criticism from Congress and the media, but it sufficiently intimidated the Blackfeet into a grudging peace with the intruders. The fatalities of the Baker Massacre were a mere pittance compared to the diseases brought by the continuing influx of settlers—diseases against which Native Americans had no natural immunity. Smallpox repeatedly ravaged many of the Plains tribes, and the Blackfeet were no exception. In 1837 alone, a severe smallpox epidemic killed approximately two-thirds of the Blackfeet population.

Red Crow (pictured here standing between two Canadian officials) served as chief of the Blood from 1870 to 1900 and helped his people become more self-sufficient during the early years of their life on Canada's largest reserve.

The same year of the Baker Massacre, the area of present-day Alberta, formerly under control of the Hudson's Bay Company, was transferred to the Canadian government in order to open the area to settlement. The government promptly made its influence known by establishing the famous North-West Mounted Police, or Mounties, to keep order in the new territory. Although the Mounties were not the Dudley Do-Rights of popular culture, their honesty and respect toward the

Blackfeet, as well as their effectiveness in eliminating the whiskey trade in Alberta, won them the regard and cooperation of the Blackfeet chiefs. In 1877, the Canadian government offered to sign a treaty with the Blackfeet that would place them on reservations (called reserves in Canada). Despite the fact that the Canadian officials dismissed any attempt to negotiate more favorable terms, Blackfeet chiefs readily agreed to sign the treaty. Apparently their willingness to sign was motivated more out of respect for the commander of the Mounties, Colonel James F. Macleod, than enthusiasm for or even understanding of the treaty itself. Red Crow, an influential Kainah chief, seems to have summed up the chiefs' thinking when he stated:

> Three years ago, when the police first came to the country, I met and shook hands with Stamixotokon [Macleod's Blackfeet name] at Belly River. Since that time he made me many promises. He kept them all—not one of them was ever broken. Everything that the police have done has been good. I entirely trust Stamixotokon, and will leave everything to him. I will sign.

A letter written in 1879 by an Oblate priest named Father Scollen who was present at the treaty agreement underscores the problems inherent in a compact made between two cultures that lacked any real understanding of one another.

> Did these Indians, or do they now, understand the real nature of the treaty made between the Government and themselves in 1877? My answer to this question is unhesitatingly negative. . . .

> It may be asked: If the Indians did not understand what the treaty meant, why did they sign it? Because previous to the treaty they had always been kindly dealt with by the Authorities, and did not wish to offend them; and although

they had many doubts in their mind as to the meaning of the treaty, yet with this precedent before them, they hoped that it simply meant to furnish them plenty of food and clothing, and particularly the former, every time they stood in need of them.

Despite this problem and the fact that the treaty had to be quickly altered to give the Kainahs, North Piegans, and Siksikas their own separate reservations, on the whole the removal of the Blackfeet to reservations was a much more peaceful process in Canada than in the United States. Bloodshed was averted in part because certain prominent chiefs espoused cooperation with the whites and because there was a significantly smaller population of white settlers in the area; but peace held primarily because Canadian authorities wished to avoid the bloody Indian Wars of its southern neighbor, and as a result, were much more likely than their U.S. counterparts to honor treaties and to treat Native Americans with something approaching respect. Relations between the Canadians and the Blackfeet became strained when the dependence and restriction of movement inherent in reserve life became apparent; however, enough goodwill remained that when a number of Native American tribes joined in an armed rebellion against the Canadians in 1885, most of the Blackfeet remained loyal to the crown.

The United States, in contrast, followed what had become its traditional policy of aggressively taking over Native American land. Treaties signed in 1865, 1888, and 1896, and executive orders signed in 1873 and 1874 moved the southern borders of Blackfeet territory ever northward. Squeezed out, hunted down, ravaged by strange diseases, and deprived of their primary food source, the South Piegans became dependent upon rations provided by the U.S. government, but this food source proved far from certain. In the winter of 1883–84, the buffalo hunts failed completely, and the U.S. government, in defiance of treaty, failed to provide the South Piegans with adequate winter rations. As a result, more than six hundred men, women, and children died in what came to be known as "Starvation Winter." This tragedy severely weakened the South Piegans and placed them firmly under the control of the only available food supplier, the U.S. government. In 1887, the General Allotment Act restricted all Blackfeet in the United States to the newly created Blackfeet Reservation in Montana. True to form, the U.S. government then demanded further capitulations of territory within the reservation, establishing its present-day boundaries in 1896. The Blackfeet, who were once free to roam an immense territory, were now entirely restricted to reservations and dependent upon governments that were completely foreign to them.

# 6

# The Blackfeet Change with the Times

S hortly after the Piegans agreed to move to a reservation, Congress passed the *Curtis Act*, which denied tribal governments sovereignty and placed Native Americans completely and solely under the control of the U.S. government. The act was not aimed at the Blackfeet in particular, but it was designed basically to force all Native Americans to assimilate into Euro-American culture, and it had a detrimental effect on the Blackfeet as well as many other Native American tribes.

Under the Curtis Act, Native Americans could be and were forbidden to follow their traditional religion, speak their native tongues, or be educated by tribal elders. Even simple ceremonies such as the baby-naming ceremony, in which a newborn is given its tribal name, were banned. In addition, the U.S. government often exercised its control over Native Americans in demeaning and provocative ways. For example, Blackfeet adults were not allowed to leave the reservation without permission from the Indian *agent* in charge, nor were any white people allowed to enter the reservation without a pass—and as late as 1908, the Blackfeet Reservation was literally fenced in to enforce this policy.

In order to keep the Blackfeet from passing on their traditions to the next generation, children were educated in government-established boarding schools located off the reservation. Many children were forcibly removed from their homes and placed in these schools, and all children in the schools were punished if they were caught singing tribal songs, doing tribal dances, or practicing any aspects of their old religion. Canada's policy toward Native Americans, codified in the 1876 Indian Act, was equally hostile toward Native customs, and the Department of Indian Affairs established both day schools on the reservations and boarding schools located off the reservations that were sponsored by the Church of England. Unlike their Montanan counterparts, many Albertan Blackfeet willingly sent their children to the boarding schools, but this was because conditions on the reservations were so harsh that such schools were often the only way parents could guarantee their children adequate food and shelter. Day schools offered no such assurance and thus were quite unpopular.

Although it lacked the missionary forces of the Church of England, the U.S. government did invite many Christian missionaries onto the reservation in the hopes of eliminating traditional (and remarkably tenacious) religious practices. The Jesuits, called "Black Robes" by the Native Americans, had been somewhat futilely involved in missions to the Blackfeet long before the tribe was placed on a reservation. After 1887, the Jesuits became a major force on the reservation, opening schools and teaching the Blackfeet how to raise cattle and how to farm. Perhaps more importantly, the Jesuits learned and preserved the Blackfeet language by translating religious texts into Blackfeet. They also served as mediators between white settlers and the Blackfeet, and facilitated treaties on their behalf, but

Siksika children read from English texts at a missionary school on their reservation in Montana. Children were often forcibly removed from their homes and forbidden to speak their language while attending these schools.

eventually their influence waned as other religions established missions and schools in the area.

Other attempts to force the Blackfeet to assimilate into white culture proved deadlier. Government officials on both sides of the border believed that the Blackfeet should give up their nomadic existence; a 1909 report by the Canadian Department of Indian Affairs claimed that by living in cabins or huts rather than tepees the Blackfeet would be taking "the first essential step towards civilization." Unfortunately, the government did not provide the Blackfeet with adequate housing, and most Blackfeet were too poor to afford anything but poorly ventilated, dark, cramped hovels that proved to be perfect breeding grounds for disease, especially tuberculosis and the eye disease trachoma. Neither government provided its reservations with adequate health care facilities or personnel, and a combination of neglect and poor nutrition ravaged the Blackfeet population. In 1916, one U.S. physician estimated that 64.3 percent of the South Piegans suffered from trachoma, while 30 percent had tuberculosis; in Canada the population of North Piegans was halved primarily due to disease between the years 1888 and 1909.

With the extermination of the buffalo, the Blackfeet needed some other form of sustenance. Both the U.S. and Canadian governments provided tribe members with rations; however, these were always at the mercy of cost-conscious government officials, and rations were also sold for personal profit by Indian agents. Programs were instituted by both governments to make the Blackfeet economically self-sufficient farmers and ranchers and to lessen their dependence on rations. However farsighted such programs may seem, they often became excuses to cut rations, weakening the Blackfeet, and not incidentally, saving the U.S. and Canadian governments money. For example, rations were withheld by U.S. officials during the disastrous Starvation Winter purportedly because the government had already spent money that year on an irrigation project that was supposed to have made the South Piegans successful farmers. Similar policies were followed in Canada, where in the early 1900s an Indian agent gave the Siksikas a onetime gift of cattle in lieu of yearly rations; when half the stock died in the severe winter of 1906–7, the agent refused to release additional rations and numerous Siksikas starved.

When economic development programs were not being used as an excuse to cut rations, they were crippled by poor management and unrealistic expectations. Most U.S. and Canadian policy-makers were agrarian idealists who believed that farming would be a "civilizing" influence as well as a means to economic independence for Native Americans. Consequently, the U.S. government was attempting to establish farms for the Blackfeet as early as 1855, but this pilot project, along with the majority of farming ventures on both sides of the border, quickly failed. Commercial agriculture was completely alien to the traditional Blackfeet way of life, and the Blackfeet had always chosen their land for its abundance of game and pasturage, not for its quality as farmland. Neither government was willing to fund the necessarily lengthy programs of agricultural education, and while both governments hired men to run educational model farms, these jobs either were doled out to incompetents in return for political favors or were given to men who already had far too many other responsibilities on the reservations to properly tend crops (One Native American historian has even said that these programs were set up with failure in mind. Former Alliance for Native American Indian Rights President Nick Mejia said in an interview: "The Indians were not supposed to survive, but to eventually perish.") Finally, the harsh climate of the area made agriculture impractical even for experienced farmers. From 1880 to 1891, more than one million white settlers in the Canadian West found the conditions there so severe that they returned to the better farmlands and milder climates of the East, but Blackfeet who attempted farming were restricted to their reserves and could not move to more amenable areas.

More success greeted attempts to develop cattle ranches on the reservations. The Blackfeet already had a tradition of caring for livestock in the form of horses, and cattle were more rugged than crops and better able to survive droughts and blizzards. In fact, white ranchers had established a booming cattle industry in Alberta by the turn of the century, often grazing their herds (legally or illegally) on the reserves and occasionally losing cows to hungry Blackfeet. But the choice between farming and cattle-raising was by no means clear to government officials, who believed that ranching lacked the civilizing influence of farming. As a result, efforts to encourage ranching were relatively intermittent and seriously underfunded in both the

United States and Canada. In addition, the Blackfeet on both sides of the border were not allowed to manage their own herds, but had to clear all such decisions with officials. Initially, this policy was enforced to prevent mismanagement of the herds, but government officials were often poor managers themselves, and the policy discouraged Blackfeet ranchers who were never allowed to feel they actually owned their herds. Despite these barriers, by the 1900s the South Piegans and especially the Kainahs were experiencing some success in their attempts to raise cattle.

But a severe blow was dealt the South Piegans when Congress passed the *Blackfeet Allotment Act* in 1907, which broke up the tribal reservation into smaller units of land that were assigned to individuals. This policy was enacted without the consent of the South Piegans, placing it in direct violation of a treaty agreement reached in 1895, in which the U.S. government promised to never break the Blackfeet Reservation up into allotments without the tribe's consent. Some individuals refused allotments, but the Bureau of Indian Affairs assigned them land plots anyway, then opened the "surplus" land—some 800,000 acres—to white settlement.

The land allotment policy was a disaster and failed miserably, not only because the Blackfeet in Montana lost hundreds of thousands of acres of land, but also because the allotments themselves were almost useless to the individuals who owned them. They were too small to herd cattle on, the climate made farming impractical, and the South Piegans lacked the funds to develop the land in other ways. The allotments could easily be sold to non-Indians, and many South Piegan landowners were swindled out of their land. Due to high rates of illiteracy and traditions that honored verbal wills, written wills were rarely used by the Blackfeet, and in their absence, land allotments were divided among the surviving relatives, resulting in land claims that were too small to support any enterprise and were often sold. In addition, the allotments were taxed, and if taxes were not paid, the land was seized by the U.S. government. The result of these dealings with South Piegan land resources was predictable; a land survey conducted in the late 1930s revealed that sales and seizures of allotments had reduced Blackfeet land holdings by 210,000 acres.

Although a form of the allotment system did exist in Canada, Canadian Blackfeet could not sell their allotments to people outside their tribe. In addition, the allotments were not taxed, and reservation land left over after the allotments were assigned remained in tribal hands instead of being opened to white settlement. The entire tribe could agree to sell their land to the Canadian government, however, and the Blackfeet were often pressured both by Canadian officials and their own dire economic conditions into giving up land, usually in return for an increase of rations. Between 1900 and 1920, the North Piegans sold a quarter of their reserve to the Canadian government, while the Siksikas surrendered fully half of their territory.

After the outbreak of World War I, several young Blackfeet men, eager for a means to fulfill the traditional role of warrior, tried to enlist in the armed forces of Canada and the United States but were actively discouraged from doing so by government officials attempting to restrict the Blackfeet to their reserves. As the war continued, the demand for manpower escalated, and some Blackfeet were allowed to enlist and served with honor in Europe. The main impact of World War I, however, was felt on the reservations, where Blackfeet poured money into the Canadian Patriotic Fund and American Liberty Bonds, while government officials began drives to increase agricultural output on reservation land to help support the war effort. Such productivity drives resulted in an increase in farming on the Montana reservation that unfortunately proved temporary; on the Kainah Reserve, however, the effect of wartime agricultural policy was much more dire. There, agents, given free use of Blackfeet resources and land thanks to wartime directives, neglected and destroyed the profitable Kainah cattle herds during the winter of 1919–20 in what many Kainahs believed was a deliberate attempt to impoverish the tribe and force them to cede territory. Some agents became rich and powerful during this time of unmitigated greed.

In part to reward Native Americans for their service in World War I, the United States granted Native Americans citizenship in 1924 (Canada did the same in 1960). Citizenship, however, could not protect the Blackfeet from the oppressive poverty the allotment system was encouraging; to help remedy this, in 1934, the U.S. Congress passed the *Indian Reorganization Act* (IRA). The IRA ended the practice of giving out allotments, protected Native American territory, allowed tribes to organize sovereign tribal governments, and provided funds for schools, credit programs, and other benefits. The South Piegans quickly took advantage of the new law, forming the Blackfeet Tribal Business Council and writing a formal constitution in 1935. In 1936, Native Americans were deemed eligible for Social Security, allowing elderly and infirm South Piegans access to a reliable source of income. Medical care also improved a great deal in the 1930s, culminating in the opening of a new hospital on the Blackfeet Reservation in 1937. Following this, Native Americans who had a vision of having more say in their lives established the National Congress of American Indians (NCAI). Founded in 1944 in Washington, D.C., NCAI's mission was to "inform the public and federal government on tribal self-government, treaty rights, and a broad range of federal policy issues affecting tribal governments." Despite these steps in progress, Blackfeet agriculture, and thus their economy, suffered as mechanized, large-scale farming became common because Blackfeet farmers generally lacked the funds necessary to purchase expensive agricultural equipment.

During World War II, many Blackfeet men and women served in the armed forces or worked in off-reservation defense plants. Both types of jobs were relatively well paying, but after the war, Blackfeet workers and soldiers returned to the reservation to discover that a labor glut had further restricted the already limited opportunities for work. Consequently, many

## Letter to President Roosevelt

In the early days of the first term of office for President Franklin D. Roosevelt, members of the Blackfeet Nation wrote him a letter. In this letter to the president and other members of his cabinet, the Blackfeet people wrote about the causes of continuing problems with the U.S. government and asked for their *own* "New Deal." In 1934, after a recommendation from the Roosevelt administration, Congress passed the Indian Reorganization Act, often referred to as the "Indian New Deal." Here are a few excerpts from the letter (with unmodified capitalization and spelling), which can be found in the National Archives and Records Administration, Washington, D.C.:

Dear Sirs:

As a member of the Blackfeet tribe a democrat and a Citizen, I desire to give voice to matters that need attention in behalf of the Indian; we too need a new deal and are not getting it. In fact, it looks as though we might lose our valuable water right and irrigation project, due to the fact of a heavy debt accumulated during the past years of Republican rule and wasteful management; we are trying to educate our children, only to see them pushed aside by outsiders from most every state in the Union.

. . . We are not just talking to find fault . . . let us have the benefit of the new democracy; Roosevelt carried the county by over 1000 votes—1717 to about 700—and the rest of you not so well but good . . . . Extend to us the helping hand and deal with us intelligently and we will reciprocate.

We congratulate you on the great success the Administration has so far made and ask that we be let into the good things to be dealt out.

Very sincerely,
[Signed, individual tribe members]

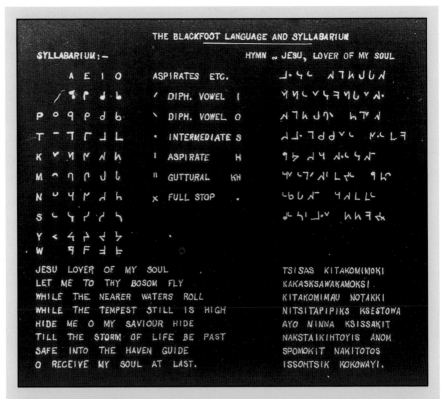

THE BLACKFOOT LANGUAGE AND SYLLABARIUM

SYLLABARIUM:—                                    HYMN — JESU, LOVER OF MY SOUL

JESU LOVER OF MY SOUL
LET ME TO THY BOSOM FLY
WHILE THE NEARER WATERS ROLL
WHILE THE TEMPEST STILL IS HIGH
HIDE ME O MY SAVIOUR HIDE
TILL THE STORM OF LIFE BE PAST
SAFE INTO THE HAVEN GUIDE
O RECEIVE MY SOUL AT LAST.

TSISAS KITAKOMIMOKI
KAKASKSAWAKAMOKSI
KITAKOMIMAU NOTAKKI
NITSITAPIPIKS KSESTOWA
AYO NINNA KSISSAKIT
NAKSTAIKIHTOYIS ANOM
SPOMOKIT NAKITOTOS
ISSOHTSIK KOKOWAYI.

In the late 1800s, the Jesuits, a Catholic order of priests, learned and preserved the Blackfeet language so that the Blackfeet could read from Christian religious texts. However, by the mid-twentieth century, the Blackfeet language had nearly been lost, because the tribe's elders had not passed the language on to younger generations. Shown here is the Blackfeet alphabet, a table of characters that represents syllables, and a translation of a Christian hymn.

people left the reservation in Montana and moved to other western states in search of work. Most of the Blackfeet who left the reservation, however, found themselves working for low wages as unskilled laborers among people who misunderstood and mocked their culture, and many eventually returned. But in the 1950s, the landholdings of the tribe eroded rapidly as the postwar population boom among non-Indians created an enormous demand for land in Montana, and Blackfeet who owned or had inherited allotments given out before 1934 sold them to non-Indians. The Blackfeet language was nearly lost as well, as the older Blackfeet who knew the language passed on without teaching it to the younger Blackfeet.

The 1960s and 1970s saw a backlash to this cultural erosion and financial exploitation. The Blackfeet in Montana began actively encouraging elders to teach the old language and the old customs to the younger generations, an effort that culminated in the publication of a Blackfeet dictionary in 1989 and a Blackfeet grammar book in 1991 by the University of Lethbridge in Alberta. Reservation housing in Montana also began to improve in the 1960s and 1970s, when several housing projects were developed. The impetus for this development was a disastrous flood that destroyed the homes of 129 families in 1964. The new homes, built with Bureau of Indian Affairs funds, were on the whole larger and sturdier than the old and demonstrated the low quality of earlier Blackfeet housing. The Blackfeet Indian Housing Authority sponsored projects such as Mutual Help Housing, where people to be housed in a particular project were required to contribute their labor to building the project, and no one was allowed to move in until the entire project was finished. This work arrangement lowered costs, provided unemployed Blackfeet with the opportunity to learn skills, and helped people build a community rather than merely shelter.

For the Canadian Blackfeet, the 1960s and 1970s were a time of great controversy. In 1969, the Canadian minister of Indian Affairs released the "Statement of the Government of Canada on Indian Policy, 1969," better known as the White Paper, which called for the abolishment of the special trust relationship between the Canadian government and the Native peoples living in Canada. Although enactment of the policies outlined in the White Paper would have guaranteed Native Americans civil liberties and autonomy in their financial affairs, it also would have eliminated any special protection of their land. The Indians of Alberta promptly responded in 1970 with a position paper of their own, entitled "Citizens Plus" (also called the Red Paper), which maintained that while the Natives of Canada deserved the full rights of citizenship, their status as aboriginal peoples gave them the additional right to claim special protection of their territory. Neither the White Paper nor the Red Paper has been adopted as Canadian policy, which has officially changed little since 1876. As a result, while the Canadian government has ceased procedures such as discouraging native religious practices, it still effectively has complete control over the disbursement of tribal funds, and it has been bitterly criticized for underfunding long-term development projects.

As with many Native American tribes—due to the loss of their natural way of life and habitat since the influx of the white man—Blackfeet have been plagued with high rates of alcoholism, suicide, and unemployment, which are all exacerbated by poverty and a lack of opportunity. Alcoholism has been a problem since its introduction to the Blackfeet by white traders in the eighteenth century. In the early 1980s, the Blackfeet Nation established alcoholism-prevention programs with the goal of eradicating alcoholism entirely. Programs aimed at young people were initiated, to teach them choice-making skills as well as outdoor and traditional skills, to kindle their imaginations, and show them they can enjoy themselves without alcohol. These early-intervention programs were not only run by the Blackfeet but used Blackfeet counselors; as one youth counselor pointed out, Native American counselors were mindful of the spiritual (not necessarily religious) aspects of the harmful effects of addiction:

> What [alcoholism] really does is kill your spirit, and even if you are functioning, you can be spiritually dead. We incorporate Indian spiritual values because the use of drugs and alcohol has brought the People to a level of guilt and shame, and we remind them that the medicine man always says that the altar is always there.

These programs were sorely needed; according to one Blackfeet alcohol-abuse therapist, by the end of the 1990s, Fetal Alcohol Syndrome (FAS) occurred in one in every one hundred births in some Indian communities, and the rate of child abuse in these communities was correspondingly high.

According to U.S. Census figures of 1990, unemployment on the Blackfeet Reservation was estimated to be between 55 percent and 64 percent. According to Jim Kennedy, former Director of Revenue for the tribe, only about 2 percent of the people living on the reservation held a college degree, and the percentage of students who dropped out of school was high. This was due in part to the fact that agricultural work, which requires little education, has historically been the largest employer on the reservation, providing little incentive for people on the reservation to put time and money into getting a college degree. But the Blackfeet began actively working to change these statistics by promoting education and programs to ensure economic opportunities to tribespeople.

Through the 1990s, farming and cattle-raising remained the two major sources of income on the reservation, and the number of Blackfeet-owned businesses began to grow both on and off the reservation. In the past, Blackfeet-owned businesses had a high rate of failure due to heavy governmental regulations, poor planning and management, and a lack of business skills among the Native American population. The Bureau of Indian Affairs, which was supposed to oversee use of the reservation in a trustee-like position, had been criticized for being too controlling and for hampering Blackfeet attempts at both economic and agricultural development. Racism was also taking its toll, both in the classroom and in the loan office. Special loans existed for Blackfeet entrepreneurs, but according to Kennedy, some unscrupulous people were "taking advantage of their Indian heritage" by lying about their intentions for the money in order to obtain funds. In addition, capitalism—

Three Kainah children stand in front of a play tepee made of flour sacks. Retaining their cultural identity has been important for Blackfeet throughout the twentieth century and will continue to be in the twenty-first century.

which often emphasizes competition, distrust, and winning at all costs—seemed at odds with traditional Blackfeet philosophies. As Native American historian Nick Mejia stated: "The European invasion was a disaster for the American Indian, since it compelled the Indian people to enter a cash economy, adopt different foods, and speak an alien language while divorcing the people from the land. Virtually every instance of communal stress can be traced to the shift from a land-based culture to one defined by consumerism and a global economy." As a result, many Blackfeet felt that, in order to succeed in mainstream American society, they were obligated to betray their values and their traditions.

Despite this internal conflict, the Blackfeet people began looking for ways to increase awareness of their culture and traditions while raising revenue. Tours of the Blackfeet Reservation thus began gaining in popularity, as more people wanted to see and experience "Native America" for themselves. Tourists visiting the reservation were often surprised to discover how similar Blackfeet life was to their own. Blackfeet people of the 1990s were practicing Catholics, Baptists, Evangelists, and Methodists, although some still practiced the traditional Blackfeet religion, and many combined practices from both religious traditions, sharing the same similarities in lifestyle as that of "mainstream" American society.

Despite these signs of assimilation, Blackfeet culture retained its separateness and uniqueness. In his book *Modern Blackfeet*, anthropologist Malcolm McFee described what he called the "Third Generation Phenomenon." Despite the pressure to assimilate and the intermarriage between whites and Native Americans, McFee predicted in 1972 that Blackfeet culture would remain strong in years to come, because

> the children of white-oriented families who have achieved a measure of economic security are taking an increased interest in Indian traditions. . . . College youth who have been taken up in the . . . student Indian movements . . . and their peers on the reservation are not only asserting their Indian identity, but their tribal identity as well.

McFee hoped that the young mixed-race Blackfeet would eliminate the social divisions of the Blackfeet community and bring greater understanding and harmony between Indians and non-Indians. McFee added that full-blooded Blackfeet

Indians who have clung tenaciously to the old ways, despite sometimes violent opposition, could give mixed-race Blackfeet a "source of identity and pride" and enrich the quality of everyone's lives.

By the end of the 1900s, the winds of change were beginning to blow in a more favorable direction for the Blackfeet and other Native American nations. The white population felt increasingly empathetic toward Native Americans' past problems and present needs. A young generation of Native Americans, now armed with college degrees, practical experience, pride in their ancestry, and a desire to help their people, began to return to the reservations they could not wait to leave in previous years.

As the twentieth century came to a close, the Blackfeet Nation looked toward the dawn of the twenty-first century with a mixture of hope, pride in their history, and anticipation for the prosperity that lay ahead.

# 7

# The Blackfeet in the Twenty-First Century

The present-day Blackfeet Reservation in the United States is located in the northwestern part of Montana, just east of Glacier National Park. It is approximately 2,400 square miles in size (or more than 1.5 million acres) and is bordered on the north by Canada, on the east by the Marias (what the Blackfeet call Two Medicine) River, on the west by the Continental Divide, and on the south by Birch Creek. The political and economic center of the reservation is the town of Browning. There are currently more than 15,000 enrolled tribal members; of these, approximately 7,000 enrolled Blackfeet live on the Montana reservation, while another 8,560 live in the three Canadian reserves around Lethbridge, Alberta. The Blackfeet, however, are not the only people living on the reservation; many non-Blackfeet Indians and non-Indians live there as well.

As it was in the 1990s, farming and raising cattle and horses are still the major sources of income on the reservation, but Blackfeet

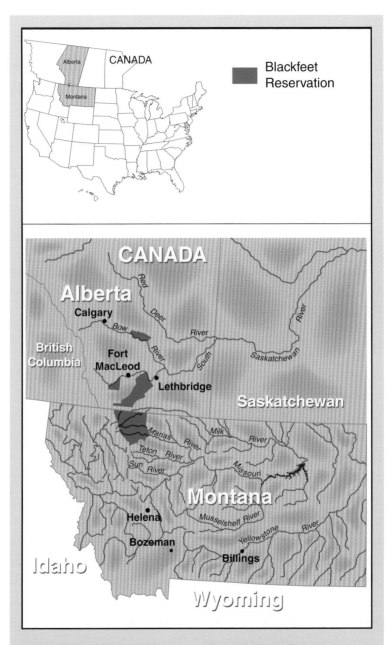

Today, there are four Blackfeet reservations: one in northwestern Montana, near Glacier National Park, and three in southern Alberta, near the town of Lethbridge.

businesses also continue to grow and flourish. With greater acknowledgement of their sovereignty, combined with increased business skills, the Blackfeet people now have more control over their own destinies, as well as economies, and they now operate many successful business ventures. Racism isn't the problem it used to be, and although it still exists, modern Blackfeet refuse to give in—or give up. Today, Blackfeet people are comfortable working in a capitalist society, while remaining true to their traditional philosophy, which emphasizes cooperation and mutual trust within the tribe. They no longer consider themselves betrayers of their tradition if they are successful entrepreneurs.

Modern Blackfeet are thus learning how to function in Western society, while remaining true to their own values. The Kainahs in Alberta run a shopping center, a newspaper, and a factory that produces prefabricated homes; and the North Piegans run garment and moccasin factories. The Blackfeet in Browning have also started a company, which is growing to be a major supplier of modular homes both on and off the reservation. Also in Montana in 2001, the Blackfeet made entrepreneurial history when they sold the assets of Blackfeet National Bank of Browning to the first nationwide American Indian bank, Native American Bancorporation (NABC). One of the founders and the former chairperson of Blackfeet National Bank is tribal member and activist Elouise Cobell, who also helped found NABC and was recently made a member of the Montana Board of Investments by Governor Brian Schweitzer. The investors of NABC are a consortium of more than a dozen Native American tribes and Alaska Native corporations. Extending their sphere of influence ever wider, some Blackfeet people have started businesses selling and servicing computer hardware and software technologies.

Native Americans, including the Blackfeet, are beginning to prosper as a result of an increase in interest in aboriginal-style artwork. The Indian Arts and Crafts Board, which is a part of the U.S. Department of the Interior, was created by Congress in order to promote the economic development of American Indians and Alaska Natives by expanding the Indian arts and crafts market. The board also administers a number of museums, including the Museum of the Plains Indian in Browning, Montana. The museum, founded in 1941, displays such cultural items as pottery, clothing, art, decorative household items, moccasins, shields, and jewelry. The top priority of the Indian Arts and Crafts Board, the only federal agency solely concerned with benefiting Native American cultural development, is to enforce the Indian Arts and Crafts Act of 1990, which criminally and civilly penalizes anyone who sells or advertises products as "Indian-made" when they are not, thereby protecting the arts and crafts market share for all Native people. Using this legislation and new venues to sell their arts and crafts, an increasing number of Blackfeet handmade crafts are now sold via the Internet, on and off the reservation, in shops, and in catalogs.

The National Congress of American Indians, mentioned in the previous chapter, has grown since its inception in 1944 to include more than 250 tribal governments from every region in the country, and today is the oldest and largest tribal government organization in the United States. The NCAI also allows individual memberships, and encourages its members to be proactive by contacting Congress and federal government agencies about issues of concern to Native people. The Blackfeet Nation has been a long-time member of the NCAI.

Tours of the Blackfeet Reservation continue to gain in popularity. Some travel agencies now specialize in tours of Native American reservations, and the Blackfeet Reservation welcomes roughly 2 million visitors a year, many of whom also tour nearby Glacier National Park. Although some tourists have denigrating and rigid ideas of what Native Americans are like, most are open-minded, appreciative, and intelligent people who wish to learn about reservation life.

Every site on the tour is full of historical significance to

The landscape of northwestern Montana was largely shaped by glaciers and was known to the Blackfeet as "the backbone of the world." In 1910, President Taft signed a bill that established our nation's tenth national park—Glacier. The 1 million-acre park shares a border with the Blackfeet Reservation to its east and the area is sacred to the tribe. Shown here is a group of Blackfeet on horseback near Cracker Lake, Glacier National Park.

both Native American and other cultural groups. Tourists can visit the area on the eastern part of the reservation called Ghost Ridge, which contains the communal burial grounds of the people who died during Starvation Winter in 1883–84. Chief Mountain, a prominent landmark that was once a sacred site for Blackfeet vision quests, can be viewed looming above Sweet Grass Hills near an entrance to the reservation. Visitors can see Two Medicine River—known as the Marias River by non-Blackfeet—near where Meriwether Lewis had his altercation

## Crisis in Glacier National Park

The mountains of Glacier National Park can attribute their dramatic beauty to glaciers. Nothing makes the heart beat quite so fast as to see the sun shining on these sheets of magnificent ice. Glaciers are also largely responsible for shaping the dramatic landscape, which led the Blackfeet to call this area "the backbone of the world," and it was known to early visitors as the "little Switzerland of America." By 1898, the Blackfeet had already sold the land to whites, and when rumors of precious metals proved false, conservationist George Bird Grinnell helped persuade Congress to establish this northern part of the Rocky Mountain chain as Glacier National Park.

Now the area Grinnell termed the "crown of the continent" is in danger.

The issue of global warming—what some thought was a mere pessimistic prediction until recently—has come to the attention of people from all over the world, but perhaps nowhere else more than those who live near Glacier National Park. Now, it is a known and measurable fact: global temperatures are shooting up, and quickly, mostly due to rising carbon dioxide ($CO_2$) emissions.

What is global warming doing to the earth? Rivers are running dry, lakes are evaporating, coastal areas are eroding, and flora and fauna are suffering in what scientists say is the fastest climate warming in the past ten thousand years.

In Glacier National Park, there are only twenty-seven glaciers of the original ninety-nine that remain, and they are shrinking at an alarmingly measurable rate. Environmentalists are so concerned that in 2004 Jeffrey Selingo wrote a piece for the *New York Times* entitled "Going to Glacier? You Should Hurry."

Now, after generations of "mainstream" Americans have ignored Native American wisdom, the First People are being consulted as to what to do to preserve the earth. From National Park Service workers to legislators, people are reconsidering the "earth-wisdom" of the Native Americans as something worthwhile after all. Unfortunately, it may be too late to reverse this tragic trend.

with the Blackfeet horse-raiding party. The river got its name after two feuding tribes held two separate Sun Dances one year. Tourists can also walk on the Old North Trail, which is believed to be part of a migration route from Asia that extends from northern Canada to Mexico and was used for centuries by Blackfeet hunters and war parties. With a grant from the Lewis and Clark Bicentennial Commission, a Blackfeet Historical Trail has also been installed on the reservation, which includes a guided tour.

There are now several good schools on the reservation, as well as gas stations, grocery stores, hardware stores, and libraries. There are also two gaming facilities, one in Cut Bank and the other in East Glacier, both of which are enjoying some success. There is a reservation-based higher-education facility, Blackfeet Community College, which has an average enrollment of more than 650 students and graduates approximately 120 students annually. As more and more Blackfeet earn college degrees (currently about 5 percent), the unemployment rate—currently at 57 percent, according to reservation-gleaned economic figures—will continue to decline.

Although problems persist, such as alcoholism and poverty, George Heavy Runner, who serves in the Blackfeet Tribal Planning Office, believes that for every problem, there is usually more than one solution. "Evolvement," he said in an interview, "is at the heart of the issue, and the issue is that poverty impacts values and living conditions." While he and many others are actively involved in serving on committees and special interest groups, such as child care, health care, and wellness, there is much to be done to improve living conditions on the reservation. Only a few decades ago the Blackfeet lived in less than desirable conditions; however, thanks in large part to the efforts of such leaders as Heavy Runner, the Blackfeet are now prospering.

A large part of the Blackfeet Nation's prosperity is also due to the leadership of Chief Earl Old Person. Old Person is a full-blooded Blackfeet who attended school on the reservation and has been involved in Blackfeet tribal government since he was a child. He has served for fifty years on the Blackfeet Tribal Business Council (forty-two of those years as chairman), was president of the National Congress of American Indians in the 1960s, and has strongly dedicated himself to promoting Native American ideals and encouraging positive intercultural relations. His effectiveness as a leader has resulted in his being honored by a number of U.S. presidents, the prime minister of Canada, and the Royal Family of England. He is also one of the people behind the movement to preserve Blackfeet culture through the preservation of their language.

Long in danger of disappearing, the Blackfeet language is making a comeback thanks in part to the efforts of Old Person, who is cochairman of the Blackfeet Language/Cultural Department. From preschool programs through high school, students are learning a language that their ancestors were beaten for speaking during the painful years of assimilation. At the college level, Blackfeet is taught through the Blackfeet Studies Program at Blackfeet Community College. Other great strides have been made to preserve the language. Darrell Robes Kipp founded the Piegan Institute in 1987, which is a private, non-profit organization that promotes the Blackfeet language. The institute opened language classes to day-care children in 1995, and in 1997, the Blackfeet language began to be exclusively taught and spoken at the institute's reservation-based Real Speak School, or, in Blackfeet, *Nitzipuhwahsin*. The institute began instructing kindergarteners through third graders and by the year 2000, they added grades four through eight. Currently, the school serves more than forty students. More than just a single school serving a handful of children, the Piegan Institute's language revitalization program has been visited by dozens of other tribal representatives from the United States and Canada, which has resulted in similar programs springing up on other reservations.

The learning of a language is more than just academic: for

elders, who still remember boarding-school beatings for using their ancestral tongue, it is a healing balm. For the youngsters, it has even saved a football game. In 2004, Blackfeet players beat another flag football team by calling all their plays in the Blackfeet language. Since the other team didn't know what the players were saying, the Blackfeet players won.

The Blackfeet people are also promoting cultural preservation in other ways. Piegan elder Joe Crow Shoe, who recently passed away (most Native Americans refer to it as "walking the spirit road"), was instrumental in starting an interpretive center for aboriginal people, which is now known as Head-Smashed-In Buffalo Jump. The center was built near the site where Native people, mostly Blackfeet, stampeded herds of buffalo to their death over a cliff, and is one of the largest, longest-used, and best-preserved of these sites in the country. Located east of the Porcupine Mountains near Fort McLeod, the interpretive center serves to educate people about the ancient wisdom of the Native elders, and there are special events with drumming, dancing, and seminars focusing on such aspects of tribal life as aboriginal medicines.

In addition to preserving culture, the Blackfeet are also making great strides to preserve and protect the land and the environment. William "Allen" Talks About, chairman of the Blackfeet tribe, has been trying to obtain funds to finance technology that would generate revenue from windpower. "We want to look at this as a national utility and not just to develop it for local consumption," he said of the project. Wendy Running Crane, administrative assistant to the Blackfeet Council, added, "The Blackfeet people have also remained environmentally responsible, resisting oil and gas exploration in culturally and/or environmentally sensitive areas of the reservation."

Another sign that better times are ahead is the growing number of nonprofit organizations coming to the aid of Native Americans. One example is the American Indian Education Foundation (AIEF). A member of National Relief Charities, the

Chief Earl Old Person, who served as Blackfeet tribal chairman from 1950 to 1988, and again from 1990 to 1998, has been an advocate for Blackfeet education. He helped establish Blackfeet Community College and currently serves as cochairman of the Blackfeet Language/Cultural Department. Thanks to his commitment to the Blackfeet, the American Civil Liberties Union of Montana presented Old Person with the Jeanette Rankin Civil Liberties Award—its highest honor—in 1998.

AIEF is one of the largest grantors of Native American college scholarships in the country, and provides such basics as school supplies and backpacks to younger students. The AIEF is such a strong supporter of college-attending Native Americans that instead of the usual 20 percent retention rate for Native Americans, 91 percent of the students whom they provide funds for continue their college education rather than dropping out.

Perhaps the most significant sign in support of preserving the culture of the Blackfeet and all Native American people is the newly constructed National Museum of the American Indian in Washington, D.C., which opened as part of the Smithsonian

Institution in September 2004. The $199 million museum is located on a 4.25-acre site just east of the National Air and Space Museum. After nearly fifteen years of planning and collaboration with tribal communities—including architect and project designer Douglas Cardinal, a member of the Blackfeet Nation—the vision has become a reality. The opening was celebrated with thousands of visitors and Native American dignitaries, including members of the Blackfeet Nation, one of whom beat the ceremonial drums that opened the ceremony. Among the museum's artwork and artifacts is a collection entitled "Window on Collections: Many Hands, Many Voices." This exhibit features thousands of artifacts, including many of Blackfeet origin, such as beaded objects, peace medals, and weaponry. Another priceless historical record is the museum's photo archives, containing approximately 160,000 images from daguerreotypes to digital images, all recounting the story of Native Americans and their culture. NMAI photo archivist Lou Stancari says that they consider themselves to be caretakers of these priceless images and not the owners of them.

As owners of their history, the Blackfeet are also increasingly asserting their claims to the basic human rights of dignity and empowerment. To help further this cause, the nonprofit Native American Rights Fund (NARF) was established in Boulder, Colorado. Since its inception in 1970, NARF's purpose has been to protect the rights of sovereign tribes, Native organizations, and individuals. NARF, which is headed by John Echohawk of the Pawnee Nation, has secured a number of victories for sovereign nations, including the *repatriation* of many ancestors' remains (and associated objects and artifacts) from display in museums to their tribes of origin for proper burial.

One of the most pressing legal issues—the largest class-action lawsuit ever filed by Native Americans against the U.S. government—currently pending is NARF's representation of Blackfeet member Elouise Pepion Cobell, who has become the face behind the Indian-trust movement. The basis of the suit,

Elouise Cobell, shown here on the Blackfeet Reservation near Browning, Montana, is the lead plaintiff in a class-action suit against the U.S. government filed by the Native American Rights Fund in 1996. The suit holds that the federal government has not made an accurate accounting of the royalties owed Native Americans for the right to take natural resources from their land.

which was filed in 1996, revolves around the U.S. government's mishandling of billions of dollars that were held in trust for 500,000 Native Americans. To better understand *Cobell v. Norton*, one must first remember the history of Indian trust funds management. In 1887, the Dawes Act (General Allotment Act) was passed by the U.S. government to allot 160 acres of land to the head of each Native American household and a trust fund was also set up to pay Native Americans royalties on the natural resources (money earned from oil, minerals, and timber) that the government took from their land. In 1934, the Indian Reorganization Act prevented further allotments, making individual Indian trusts perpetual. However, from the time the Dawes Act was passed, the Bureau of Indian Affairs mismanaged the money and the suit was filed to discover exactly where the money went.

In 1992, the House Committee on Government Operations issued a report, entitled "Misplaced Trust: The Bureau of Indian Affairs' Mismanagement of the Indian Trust Fund," which documented the mismanagement of tribal trust assets. Two years later, ostensibly in an attempt to repair the accounting system, Congress passed the Indian Trust Fund Management Reform Act. This was followed in 1996 by NARF's lawsuit that charged the Department of the Interior and Treasury with breaching their "fiduciary duties" (ones founded on faith or trust) by not complying with the Indian Trust Fund Management Reform Act, and that instead the agencies were continuing to mismanage trust funds and failing to repair the accounting system.

In 1999, the then Secretary of the Interior Bruce Babbitt, Treasury Secretary Robert Rubin, and Kevin Gover, assistant secretary of Indian Affairs, were all found in contempt of court because they could not produce court-ordered records supporting their defense. After a seven-week trial, and after Babbitt's admittance that the "fiduciary responsibilities" of the United States were "not being fulfilled," Judge Royce C. Lamberth ruled that the United States had "unreasonably delayed" trust reform efforts.

One might think that Lamberth's ruling resulted in a victory for NARF and the end of the story, but this ruling was followed by an appeal. Although the Federal Appeals Court upheld Judge Lamberth's ruling in February 2001, the legal battle raged on: The new secretary of the interior, Gale Norton, was accused of having inadequate computer security, which made it possible for outsiders to hack into the Individual Indian Monies trust records. After receiving court approval, attorney Alan Balaran proved how easy it was to access these records. The computer system was then shut down, and four months passed, during which time no checks were sent out by the Individual Indian Money (IIM) trust—more than 43,000

Native American landowners received no trust payments from November 2001 through February 2002.

Another ruling in 2002 by Lamberth resulted in Norton and Assistant Secretary Neal McCaleb being held in contempt of court on four of five counts, following a class-action suit that was filed holding them in contempt for allowing destruction of IIM documents as a cover-up of not only the lack of security for the technology system but also for overall mismanagement of funds. In 2003, the Federal Appeals Court reversed the contempt ruling against Norton and McCaleb but upheld Lamberth's orders to reform the trust.

A new twist is that in 2004, President George W. Bush signed into law the American Indian Probate Reform Act, authored by Senator Ben Nighthorse Campbell (Cheyenne) and supported by Secretary of the Interior Norton. This new law may finally facilitate the consolidation of Indian land ownership, and although according to NARF it will not affect the Cobell case, it is nonetheless a major step for Indian trust reform.

The case of *Cobell v. Norton* may go on for years, but in the meantime, the Blackfeet people continue to thrive. As George Heavy Runner said in an interview, "We Blackfeet have survived because we have always had a sense of humor. If it weren't for that, we couldn't laugh; and if we couldn't laugh, we wouldn't be here today."

"Being here today" includes a revival and renewed interest in traditional ways and culture. One of the most successful efforts of the Blackfeet to revive their old ways and preserve their culture is the annual North American Indian Days celebration, which is essentially a big *powwow*. Open to Indians and non-Indians alike, the Blackfeet powwow—held in Browning, Montana, for four days during the second week in July—is one of the largest on the continent. People come from all over the country and the world to watch and to participate in the celebration, camping in recreational vehicles, tents, and even tepees, while engaging in dancing, dance contests, storytelling, drum-playing, and games. Traditional Plains Indian foods, such as boiled potatoes, boiled beef and venison, sarvisberry soup, bannock bread (baking powder bread), and fry bread are served. Besides simply having a good time at these powwows, the Blackfeet hope to promote and instill in Anglo-American society a greater appreciation for their culture. The powwow lasts four days, the traditional length of a vision quest, in the hopes that all the people who attend the festival come away with a bright new vision of a future where different cultures and different races are equally appreciated, valued, and respected.

# The Blackfeet at a Glance

| | |
|---:|:---|
| **Tribe** | Blackfeet |
| **Culture Area** | Northern Great Plains |
| **Geography** | Montana, Idaho, Wyoming, Alberta, British Columbia, Saskatchewan |
| **Linguistic Family** | Algonquian |
| **Current Population (2000)** | Approximately 7,000 on Montana reservation; 8,560 on Canadian reserves |
| **First European Contact** | French fur traders; perhaps Pierre Gaultier de Varennes sieur de la Vérendrye, 1740s–50*. |
| **Federal Status** | Tribal reservation near Browning, Montana; three Canadian reserves around Lethbridge, Alberta |

* Though the individual who first encountered the Blackfeet may not be known, French fur traders set up trading posts along the branches of the Saskatchewan River and were probably the first people of European descent to encounter the Blackfeet.

>13000 B.C.   The great Native American migration from Asia.

c. 500 B.C.   Blackfeet settle in the northern Great Plains area.

c. A.D. 1750   Arrival of the horse to the northern Great Plains.

1787   David Thompson, trader/explorer, lives among the Piegans.

1804–1806   Meriwether Lewis and William Clark, with their "Corps of Discovery," explore the West.

1820–1830   Intense trapping in Blackfeet territory disrupts Blackfeet life.

c. 1830s   German prince Arthur Philip Maximilian visits area; brings artist Carl Bodmer to record tribal life.

1832–1840   American artist George Catlin visits more than forty tribes, including the Blackfeet, and paints hundreds of scenes depicting and recording most aspects of Native American life.

1830s–1850s   Smallpox epidemics ravage Blackfeet populations—a disease brought by settlers, against which Blackfeet have no natural immunities.

1840s   The "Great Emigration" of settlers into traditional Blackfeet territory.

1850s   Gold discovered in the Rocky Mountains.

1851   Treaty of Fort Laramie.

1855   Lamed Bull's Treaty, the first mutually recognized treaty between the Blackfeet and the U.S. government, is agreed upon.

1860s   Transcontinental Railroad constructed.

c. 1860–1870   Female warriors Running Eagle, Throwing Down, and Elk Hollering in the Water become legendary figures.

1860–1885   Buffalo herds dwindle to near extinction, due to white man's slaughter and competition with settlers' herds for grazing lands.

1865–1896    U.S. government creates a number of "treaties" that deprive Blackfeet of more and more of their land.

1870    The Baker Massacre; Alberta, formerly under control of the Hudson's Bay Company, transferred to Canadian governmental control—the area is then opened to settlement by whites.

1877    Canada-Blackfeet treaty is agreed upon; Canadian Department of Indian Affairs establishes on-reservation day schools and off-reservation boarding schools in an attempt to assimilate young Blackfeet.

1883–1884    "Starvation Winter" in which more than six hundred Piegans die due to failure of the U.S. government to provide food as promised through treaties.

1887    General Allotment Act (Dawes Act) restricts all Blackfeet to the newly created Blackfeet Reservation in Montana; because communal ownership of reservation land is also abolished, the tribe loses more than 800,000 acres.

1898    Congress passes the Curtis Act, denying tribal governments sovereignty and places all Native Americans completely under the control of the U.S. government.

1900–1920    North Piegans sell a quarter of their reserve, and Siksikas fully half, to the Canadian government.

1906–7    Cattle given to the Siksikas as a onetime gift in lieu of rations die in the severe winter; many Siksikas also die of starvation as a result.

1919–1920    Kainahs lose cattle herds during this hard winter; agents neglect to care for the people's needs.

1924    U.S. grants Native Americans citizenship.

1930s    Blackfeet land holdings reduced by an additional 210,000 acres, seized by the U.S. government.

1934    Congress passes Indian Reorganization Act, providing some relief to the oppressed Blackfeet—the beginning of attempts to protect tribal lands and recognize sovereign tribal governments.

1935    The first Blackfeet constitution is drawn up by the South Piegans.

1936    Native Americans deemed eligible for Social Security.

1941    Museum of the Plains Indian opens in Browning, Montana.

1944    National Congress of American Indians is founded in Washington, D.C.

1960    Canada grants Native Americans citizenship.

1960s–1970s    Blackfeet language and culture begins a reemergence among the people.

1969    Canada releases its "Statement of the Government of Canada on Indian Policy," also called The White Paper.

1970    Canadian Blackfeet publish a position paper in response, entitled "Citizens Plus," also called The Red Paper; neither paper is adopted as official policy; Native American Rights Fund, a watchdog-for-tribal-justice legal group, is founded in Boulder, Colorado.

1978    Earl Old Person earns lifetime appointment as honorary chief of Blackfeet Nation.

1989, 1991    University of Lethbridge, Alberta, Canada, publishes the first Blackfeet dictionary and grammar book.

1990    Indian Arts and Crafts Act is established in an effort to promote and protect Native cultural development and economics; U.S. Census figures record unemployment on the Blackfeet Reservation between 55 and 64 percent, with only 2 percent holding a college degree, and elevated high-school dropout rates.

1996    Original complaint of *Cobell v. Norton* filed in U.S. District Court, Washington, D.C., seeking reform of the trust system and accounting of money ostensibly held in the trust; case still pending as of 2005.

2001    Blackfeet sell assets of Blackfeet National Bank of Browning to the first nationwide American Indian bank, Native American Bancorporation.

**2004** National Museum of the American Indian, Washington, D.C., opens in September.

**2005** Blackfeet Community College thrives, graduating more than 650 students annually. Unemployment is at approximately 57 percent, with currently 5 percent of the population holding a college degree, and the Blackfeet people seem to be making a comeback.

# GLOSSARY

**agent**—A person appointed by the Bureau of Indian Affairs to supervise U.S. government programs on a reservation and/or in a specific region.

**anthropologist**—A scientist who studies human beings and their cultures.

**archaeologist**—A scientist who studies the material remains of past human cultures.

**band**—A loosely organized group of people who are bound together by the need for food and defense, by family ties, and/or by other common interests.

**Blackfeet Allotment Act**—The 1907 federal law that divided reservation land into small allotments assigned to individual families and sold the surplus to whites. This policy undermined the traditional Native way of life.

**Bureau of Indian Affairs (BIA)**—A federal government agency, now within the Department of the Interior, founded to manage relations with Native American tribes.

**calumet**—A peace pipe smoked at the agreement of treaties and carried by messengers of peace from one tribe to another.

**counting coup**—A system of ranking acts of bravery in war.

**Creator Sun**—In Blackfeet mythology, the supernatural being who created the world.

**culture**—The learned behavior of humans; nonbiological, socially taught activities; the way of life of a group of people.

**Curtis Act**—A federal law that placed Native Americans completely under the control of the U.S. government. The law was used to force the Blackfeet to assimilate into white culture, forbidding Native Americans to practice their traditional religion and speak their Native language.

**esoteric**—Relating to knowledge restricted to a small, specially initiated group.

**Indian Reorganization Act (IRA)**—The 1934 federal law that ended the policy of allotting plots of land to individuals and encouraged the development of reservation communities. The act also provided for the creation of autonomous tribal governments.

**Napi (or Old Man)**—Another name for the Creator in Blackfeet creation stories.

**peace chief**—A respected leader who settled disputes, set policy, and kept a record of the tribe's history.

**repatriation**—Returning human remains, funerary objects, and other artifacts to the rightful ancestral owners.

**reservation**—A tract of land retained by North American Indians for their own occupation and use; called a reserve in Canada.

**shaman**—A holy man who provides physical and spiritual healing for the tribe.

**Sun Dance**—A sacred ritual performed every summer in which the Blackfeet give thanks for good fortune by performing different acts. In the most dramatic facet of the ritual, men pierce their flesh with a skewer attached by a thong to a pole and dance around the pole, singing their personal songs and blowing their eagle-wing-bone whistles, until the dancers tear free.

**sweat bath**—A ritual purification in a heated lodge filled with steam, often undertaken as preparation for contact with supernatural beings.

**talisman**—An object believed to protect or bring good fortune to whomever carries it. The Blackfeet discovered many of their talismans through vision quests.

**treaty**—A contract negotiated between nations that deals with the cessation of military action, the surrender of political independence, the establishment of boundaries, the terms of land sales, and related matters.

**tribe**—A society consisting of several separate communities united by kinship, culture, language, and other social institutions, including clans, religious organizations, and warrior societies.

**vision quest**—A sacred ritual in which a person, spiritually purified through a sweat bath, experiences four days of fasting and praying in order to receive visions from a supernatural spirit who acts as a personal guardian.

**war chief**—A respected warrior who planned battle strategy and led the warriors during times of conflict.

## Books

Bullchild, Percy. *The Sun Came Down: The History of the World as My Blackfeet Elders Told It*. New York: Harper & Row, 1985.

Cantor, George. *North American Indian Landmarks: A Traveler's Guide*. Detroit, Mich.: Visible Ink Press, 1993.

Clark, Ella E. *Indian Legends from the Northern Rockies*. Norman, Okla.: University of Oklahoma Press, 1988.

Dempsey, Hugh A. *Charcoal's World*. Lincoln, Nebr.: University of Nebraska Press, 1978.

———. *Crowfoot: Chief of the Blackfeet*. Norman, Okla.: University of Oklahoma Press, 1972.

———. *Red Crow, Warrior Chief*. Lincoln, Nebr.: University of Nebraska Press, 1980.

Farr, William. *Reservation Blackfeet: 1882–1945*. Seattle, Wash.: University of Washington Press, 1986.

Grinnell, George Bird. *Blackfoot Lodge Tales: The Story of a Prairie People*. Lincoln, Nebr.: University of Nebraska Press, 1962.

Hungry Wolf, Adolph. *The Blood People: A Division of the Blackfoot Confederacy*. New York: Harper & Row, 1977.

Hungry Wolf, Beverly. *The Ways of My Grandmothers*. New York: Quill, 1982.

Lancaster, Richard. *Piegan*. Garden City, N.Y.: Doubleday, 1966.

McClintock, Walter. *Old Indian Trails*. 1923. Reprint. Boston, Mass.: Houghton Mifflin, 1992.

McFee, Malcolm. *Modern Blackfeet: Montanans on a Reservation*. New York: Holt, Rinehart & Winston, 1972.

Rosier, Paul C. *Rebirth of the Blackfeet Nation, 1912–1954*. Lincoln, Nebr.: University of Nebraska Press, 2001.

Scriver, Bob. *The Blackfeet: Artists of the Northern Plains*. Kansas City, Mo.: Lowell Press, 1990.

Taylor, Colin F. *The Plains Indians.* Avenel, N.J.: Crescent Books, 1994.

Walton, Ann T., John C. Ewers, and Royal B. Hassrick. *After the Buffalo Were Gone: The Louis Warren Hill, Sr., Collection of Indian Art.* St. Paul, Minn.: Northwest Area Foundation, 1985.

## Websites

Aboriginal Multi-Media Society (has more than twelve thousand full-text articles with searchable archives)
*http://www.ammsa.com*

American Indian Education Foundation
*http://www.aiefprograms.org*

The Blackfeet Nation
*www.blackfeetnation.com*

Intertribal Bison Cooperative
*www.intertribalbison.org*

Lewis & Clark–Blackfeet Indians
*www.nationalgeographic.com/ lewisandclark/record_tribes_005_ 19_20.html*

The National Museum of the American Indian
*www.americanindian.si.edu*

Native American News
*www.indianz.com*

Native American Rights Fund
*http://www.narf.org*

National Native American News Source
*www.indiancountry.com*

# INDEX

# INDEX

# PICTURE CREDITS

page:

2: Image # 2A-20323, Photo by Walter McClintock, American Museum of Natural History

10: Image # 2537573, Photo by Walter McClintock, American Museum of Natural History

14: Smithsonian Institution

18: Smithsonian Institution

26: Library of Congress, LC-USZ62-106274

30: Image #319798, Alex J. Rota, American Museum of Natural History Library

33: © Stapleton Collection/CORBIS

42: Image # 122751, Photo by Walter McClintock, American Museum of Natural History

47: Library of Congress, LC-USZ62-38862

51: Glenbow Archives, Calgary, Alberta

60: Glenbow Archives, Calgary, Alberta

66: Glenbow Archives, Calgary, Alberta

73: Glenbow Archives, Calgary, Alberta

77: Glenbow Archives, Calgary, Alberta

81: © Peter Lamb

84: Louis W. Hill Papers, James J. Hill Reference Library, St. Paul, Minnesota

89: Associated Press, AP

91: Associated Press, AP

A: Provincial Museum of Alberta, Canada

B: H89.220.233, Ethnology Program, Provincial Museum of Alberta, Canada

C: H65.191.3, Ethnology Program, Provincial Museum of Alberta, Canada

D: H89.220.289b, H67.317.3, H64.1.665, Ethnology Program, Provincial Museum of Alberta, Canada

E: H69.63.1a,b, Ethnology Program, Provincial Museum of Alberta, Canada

F: H89.220.136, Ethnology Program, Provincial Museum of Alberta, Canada

G: H66.312.1, Ethnology Program, Provincial Museum of Alberta, Canada

H: H68.55.31, Ethnology Program, Provincial Museum of Alberta, Canada

Cover:   H68.57.31, Ethnology Program, Provincial Museum of Alberta, Canada

**Theresa Jensen Lacey** is author of more than seven hundred articles for newspapers and magazines, a contributor to Chicken Soup for the Soul books, and has published several other books, including *The Pawnee* in the INDIANS OF NORTH AMERICA series. Lacey is of Cherokee and Comanche descent, a Charter Member of the National Museum of the American Indian, and a member of Western Writers of America. Lacey is also a teacher and has a master's degree in education. For more information on Lacey's work, access her website at *www.tjensenlacey.com*.

**Ada E. Deer** is the director of the American Indian Studies program at the University of Wisconsin–Madison. She was the first woman to serve as chair of her tribe, the Menominee Nation, the first woman to head the Bureau of Indian Affairs in the U.S. Department of the Interior, and the first American Indian woman to run for Congress and secretary of state of Wisconsin. Deer has also chaired the Native American Rights Fund, coordinated workshops to train American Indian women as leaders, and championed Indian participation in the Peace Corps. She holds degrees in social work from Wisconsin and Columbia.